What people are saying abou

LIKE JESUS

"You will find this book to be practical, enjoyable, and helpful. Living like Jesus has to be the rally cry for all Christians everywhere, and this book will help all of us do that by identifying the ways we miss out on the real Jesus and by helping us understand why the real thing is so much better than anything we could make up on our own."

Kyle Idleman, teaching pastor of
Southeast Christian Church

"It's important for us, as Christians, to make certain we are not only following Jesus faithfully but that the Jesus we are following is the One we find in Scripture. Jamie's book will help us see Him clearly and follow Him closely, as we live out His commission to make disciples."

Dave Stone, senior pastor of
Southeast Christian Church

"If you think you know who Jesus is, quite possibly you are about to have your mind stretched, presuppositions exploded, and heart expanded with this challenging, compelling, and life-giving book from Jamie Snyder."

Gene Appel, senior pastor of Eastside
Christian Church, Eastside.com

"Over the years, God has used Jamie's writing to challenge me and change me. This book is no different. Each chapter stepped on my toes and opened my eyes to see who I am in light of who Jesus is, so I hope every person in every church reads it."

Jon Weece, author of *Jesus Prom* and *Me Too*

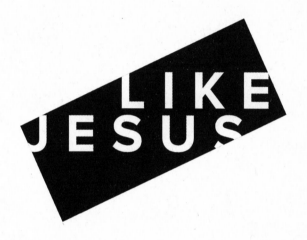

LIKE
JESUS

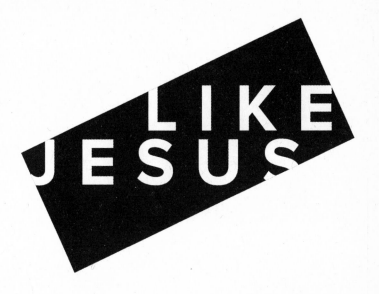

LIKE JESUS

SHATTERING OUR
FALSE IMAGES OF
THE REAL CHRIST

JAMIE
SNYDER

David C Cook®
transforming lives together

LIKE JESUS
Published by David C Cook
4050 Lee Vance View
Colorado Springs, CO 80918 U.S.A.

David C Cook Distribution Canada
55 Woodslee Avenue, Paris, Ontario, Canada N3L 3E5

David C Cook U.K., Kingsway Communications
Eastbourne, East Sussex BN23 6NT, England

The graphic circle C logo is a registered trademark of David C Cook.

The website addresses recommended throughout this book are offered as a
resource to you. These websites are not intended in any way to be or imply an
endorsement on the part of David C Cook, nor do we vouch for their content.

Unless otherwise noted, all Scripture quotations are taken from the Holy Bible, New
International Version®, NIV®. Copyright © 1973, 2011 by Biblica, Inc.® Used
by permission of Zondervan. All rights reserved worldwide. www.zondervan.com.
Scripture quotations marked MSG are taken from *THE MESSAGE*. Copyright © by
Eugene H. Peterson 1993, 2002. Used by permission of NavPress Publishing Group.

LCCN 2015942006
ISBN 978-0-7814-1136-3
eISBN 978-0-7814-1427-2

© 2016 Jamie Snyder

The Team: Alex Field, Ingrid Beck, Keith Wall, Amy
Konyndyk, Tiffany Thomas, Susan Murdock
Cover Design: Nick Lee
Cover Photo: Shutterstock

Printed in the United States of America
First Edition 2016

1 2 3 4 5 6 7 8 9 10

113015

CONTENTS

Prologue
DISCOVER OR DOWNLOAD?

Truth is discovered, not downloaded.

Those words often roll off the tongue of a dear friend of mine. Though repetitious with this phrase, he is also right, especially in regard to Jesus.

My simple hope is that as you read through these pages, you will find yourself discovering, or perhaps rediscovering, truth. By truth, I do not mean a *what*; I mean a *who*. That *who* is Jesus.

Jesus said, "I am the way and the truth and the life" (John 14:6). Discovering Jesus is not a once-in-a-lifetime event—it is an endeavor that lasts a lifetime. So use this book as an opportunity to continue that journey of discovery. Perhaps it has been some time since you have intentionally thought about who Jesus is, what He is like, what He has called you to, and, last but not least, which Jesus you have been following.

I would guess that last phrase captured your attention. If it didn't, it probably should have. Which Jesus have you been following? The question sounds ironic because, after all, isn't there only one Jesus? There is only one real Jesus, but there are many others—counterfeit

Jesuses. These counterfeit versions are built in the privacy of our hearts and minds, and they are built to resemble those who conceive them—namely, you and me. But Jesus, the real Jesus of the Bible, will never settle to imitate. Instead, He—Real Jesus—demands to be imitated. He said so, using two simple words: "Follow Me."

Jesus is not content for you to like Him; He wants you to *become* like Him. Are you? Will you? The truth awaits. He is waiting with open arms.

Part I
IMITATION

1
LIKE JESUS

"I like Jesus. I just don't like His followers."

Those words have been etched on my heart and mind since the moment I first read them. They appeared on a bumper sticker, plastered to the car in front of me at a red light. Reading the words again and again during the next few minutes, I felt sickened, frustrated, and offended. I wanted to look away, but I simply couldn't.

My response then—and my response now—was an attempt to rationalize away the bumper sticker's message. I would have loved to forget about it and move on with life; after all, I see dozens of slogans and sayings emblazoned on vehicles every day. But I could not forget that sticker, no matter how hard I tried. In fact, I took the intended meaning of the sticker quite personally. How could I not? I am a follower of Jesus. And as comfortable as it would be to dismiss those stinging words outright, doing so would be irresponsible, if not foolish.

I can't help but wonder what went wrong in the car owner's experience with Jesus's followers; clearly something had rankled the person.

I have seen only one such bumper sticker in my life, but many people have the same words etched on their hearts and minds. I don't think this negative impression is formed by one encounter with a follower of Jesus. Nor do I think this impression is formed overnight. This bitter, heartbreaking portrait of Jesus's followers is painted one brushstroke at a time.

Brushstroke: An adolescent girl, struggling to understand her sexuality, endures the pain of listening to her Christian friends mock lesbians, unaware of her struggle and confusion.

Brushstroke: A middle-aged man attends a church service for the first time in thirty years. As he kills time before the service, he stands outside the front door and smokes a cigarette, pretending to ignore the condescending stares and whispers as the members walk by.

Brushstroke: A single mom with three kids searches to find her place in the local church, but it becomes clear there is no place for someone like her. She doesn't feel welcome among the seemingly perfect couples with their seemingly perfect children.

Brushstroke: A college student from a certain minority group tries diligently to get involved in the campus ministry. He has learned to overlook skin color, but obviously the others involved have not.

Brushstroke: An impoverished family shows up at the church down the street and can't help but notice they are underdressed compared to everyone else. No one says anything to them, but the silence and pitying looks say it all.

The brushstrokes happen one at a time, but collectively they form a portrait that isn't pretty—it's quite ugly, in fact.

I wish I could say I struggled to come up with such scenarios, but the real struggle was narrowing down the examples to use.

Unfortunately, I could easily place names of real people into each one of these scenarios.

I am not suggesting that all followers of Jesus are responsible for the unappealing impression many people have of Christians. But there is no denying the impression is real. Even if it were possible to do so, pointing fingers of blame would miss the point and purpose of coming face-to-face with this harsh reality. The better approach is for those of us who claim to be Christ-followers to look honestly at ourselves and to answer some hard questions.

After much wrestling with these uncomfortable realities, I have come to this gut-wrenching conclusion: the reason so many people do not like followers of Jesus is that they are not like Jesus.

By *they*, I mean *we*.

And by *we*, I mean *I*.

How about you—are you like Jesus?

That is not a fair question. It's like asking if you love paying taxes or if you crave brussels sprouts. There is almost no one who could honestly answer yes to these questions. The same is true in asking and answering, "Are you like Jesus?" If you answer affirmatively, it indicates one of two things: either you don't know Jesus well or you don't know yourself well. No one can claim, accurately and honestly, to be like Jesus. Mother Teresa couldn't and neither could Billy Graham. Not even your grandma, though I am sure she is kind and loving.

No one can claim to be like Jesus, because doing so suggests the attainment of absolute spiritual maturity and sensitivity. Therefore, the question I have posed needs to be altered a bit or this discussion will be over before it begins. So let me add one word in the middle of the question: Are you *becoming* like Jesus?

Becoming points in a definite direction. A seed planted in the ground is becoming a tree. A caterpillar inside of a cocoon is becoming a butterfly.

The image of transformation is woven throughout the New Testament. Many times, Paul used variations of the Greek word *morphe*. You don't have to be a Greek scholar to recognize that word. The English word *metamorphosis* is derived from it. In our vernacular, we use it as a verb: "That couch potato morphed into a superstar athlete!"

There's good reason the New Testament is replete with references to metamorphosis. At the core of the Christian faith is the promise, and the expectation, of transformation, which is a matter of becoming. It is not an event, not a moment in time, but a process.

AN INVITATION TO IMITATION

Everyone, everywhere, is becoming more like someone or something. The question is, what or whom? This question may feel abstract, but it is not. In fact, this question is quite concrete and the answer should be as well. As uncomfortable as this may sound, if you struggle to determine whether you are becoming like Jesus, you probably aren't.

Some things you can accidentally become: overweight, lazy, vain, or addicted to anything from alcohol to work. These are all things we have to intentionally resist becoming, because we can inadvertently become these things if we're not careful. But becoming like Jesus is an hourly, daily, weekly, monthly commitment one makes. It is intentional. The art of imitation often is.

Perhaps this idea of imitating Jesus, or becoming like Jesus, seems foreign to you. Perhaps when you began following Jesus, no one mentioned anything about imitating Jesus. When you raised your hand or prayed the prayer or signed the card or walked to the front of the church, it was simply about making a commitment to *like Jesus*, but not necessarily to *be like Jesus*.

Perhaps there is confusion over the invitation Jesus has extended to us.

We've all heard salvation described as "accepting Christ," right? But the truth is, that's not the invitation we've been given. We don't have that power, and we don't play that role. I know some could say this is just semantics, but the words we use communicate the thoughts we think.

Here's what I mean: "Accepting Jesus" communicates clearly that at some point in time, He was allowed to enter into your world. He was added to your schedule. He was put on your calendar. He was asked to pull up a seat to your table.

Jesus has never asked anyone to accept Him, nor will He ever do so. Jesus is not the last kid on the playground holding up a hand, hoping to be picked for the kickball team. He is not the kid at the dance standing along the edges, just wishing someone would invite him out onto the dance floor. He is not the puppy at the pound that pants and squeals and wags his tail as people peruse the aisles, hoping someone will finally pick him. You get the point. Jesus is not in need of being accepted. But you are. And so am I.

Thank God, literally, that the acceptance we need is available, and it begins and ends with an invitation. It's an invitation to follow and to imitate. If the idea of imitation was lost in translation in your conversion experience, I am sorry. But following Jesus has always been about imitation. As you trace Jesus's ministry through the gospels of Matthew, Mark, Luke, and John, you will never find Jesus actually saying, "Imitate Me." Instead, you will find Him giving this invitation: "Follow Me." It's a phrase that loses a lot in translation, not so much linguistically as culturally. When someone invites you to follow him or her, it likely involves a hop, skip, and jump across the room or across the street or across the town. "Follow me" these days is an invitation that usually carries little weight and calls for little commitment. But in Jesus's day, those words were an invitation that carried lots of weight and called for lots of commitment. "Follow me" is a statement a rabbi would often make to a prospective student. The invitation was given only after a thorough assessment of the student's intentions and abilities. Tests were given, knowledge evaluated, motives questioned, and ability measured. Following a rabbi was not for the faint of heart, and so not everyone was given the invitation. Only after a long period of evaluation would a rabbi speak these words to a student: "Come, follow me." When those words were spoken, the student's life would never be the same. A decision to follow a rabbi was a decision to abandon the previous life and fully engage in the new life. There was no room in the new life to be concerned or consumed with responsibilities and pressures from the old life. The life of being a disciple was about being completely focused on the new task at hand: becoming like the rabbi. When a rabbi said, "Follow me," the words were laden with expectations. In essence, the rabbi meant, "Go where I go. Do what I do. Be like me." In other words, always and in all ways, "Imitate me." And the true disciples did.

It is said that some disciples would even follow their rabbi into the restroom because they didn't want to miss anything. Sounds extreme if you ask me, but that is simply a reflection of their commitment to imitation. Disciples would often follow so closely in the footsteps of their rabbi that a phrase came into use: "covered in the dust of the rabbi." The expression was derived from the imagery of a rabbi showing up in town, followed so closely by his disciples that they were covered in the road dust kicked up by his sandals. Following their new rabbi was not a priority of their lives; it was their *only* priority.

Disciples wanted to learn from their rabbi, but more than anything else, they wanted to *be like* their rabbi. In the Scriptures, Jesus is referred to as a rabbi. His followers were called disciples. You get the picture. Imitating Jesus is not an aspect of following Jesus; it is *the* aspect of following Jesus. As Christians, we are not merely called to *like* Jesus; we are called to *be like* Jesus.

2
BUILD-A-JESUS

I'll never forget the phone call. Afterward, tears were shed. Hugs were exchanged. My family would never be the same again.

My son had been invited to his first Build-A-Bear birthday party. I know, you were expecting something more earth shattering than an invite to stuff, dress, and overpay for a bear. But in the life of a kindergartner, this was reason to shout, skip, and celebrate. And so we did.

I still remember the day when Cy came home with the bear he had created. Carrying the box that held his new friend, he walked with a bounce in his step and a proud smile stretched wide. This wasn't just a bear—this was *his* bear, made precisely to his preferences and desires. He pulled out Felix to introduce him to the family. The bear was dressed in black pants, a white shirt, and red suspenders, though there were endless options for how he could have been attired. Every kid who had attended the party brought home a bear different from all the others. The only thing the bears had in common was that they had all been poked, pulled, dressed, accessorized, and stuffed. Poor bears.

BUILD-A-JESUS

Jesus knows the feeling. Well, kind of. As irreverent as it sounds, we live in a Build-A-Jesus spiritual climate. I know many people—perhaps including you—are offended by this statement. Yet most Christians—perhaps including you—have built their own Jesus. The building has not taken place in a brightly colored store in the local mall, but He has been built nonetheless. By me, by you, by almost everyone who has adopted the name *Christian*. It happens within the privacy of our hearts and minds.

Sort of like the kids with their fuzzy bears, we stuff, dress, and decorate Jesus to match our every desire, and then we put Him in a spiritual box and He becomes our Jesus. If you listen closely to discussions and take inventory of your own opinions, perceptions, and behaviors, it won't take long to notice that your Jesus and everyone else's Jesuses don't always match up. Not just two or three supposed Jesuses are working in collaboration with one another—or perhaps in competition with one another—there are many.

American Jesus

This Build-A-Jesus has exactly three favorite colors: red, white, and, you guessed it, blue. If He built a home, it would have three bedrooms, two baths, at least one flat-screen HDTV, and an attached two-car garage. The house would be surrounded by a white picket fence, and hanging from the porch post would be a large American flag. His favorite holiday is the Fourth of July, and every time that day rolls around, He is reminded why America is His favorite country on the planet. Abundant wealth, endless opportunities, and plentiful freedoms—how could it not be His favorite?

American Jesus weaves together words of faith and patriotism so tightly you may conclude they are one and the same. In fact, to the American Jesus, they are. To be American is to be Christian. When American Jesus's followers pray about wars, they use His own words: "May Your will be done on earth as it is in heaven." Those words are certainly admirable, but used in that context they actually mean, "May America win this war." When American Jesus's followers think about God's kingdom here on earth, they primarily think in terms of the Lower 48, with Hawaii and Alaska graciously included.

What's more, American Jesus is primarily concerned about the health and wealth of His followers. In other words, His desires align perfectly with the promises and possibilities of the American dream. With hard work and determination, you too can live a life of abundance—and why not? You deserve it. Following American Jesus will lead to more digits in your salary, more square footage in your house, more creature comforts, and a more prestigious position in your chosen vocation.

Political Jesus

This Jesus flexes His supernatural muscle at the voting polls. He works the crowd at rallies and travels the campaign trail. His effort is significant, and the work is not easy, but He does so because He believes politics is a way to achieve His ultimate objectives. Not only does He speak in support of specific candidates, but He is also quick to undermine opposing candidates. He encourages a do-whatever-it-takes approach to getting the right men and women in office, whether that is the Oval Office or the local mayoral office.

Political Jesus preaches that voting is more than an opportunity for His followers; it is also a responsibility. His presence becomes most pronounced at the end of every four-year cycle, as the presidential race ensues. In the meantime, He spends much of His time studying proposed legislation, passing petitions, registering people to vote, and pushing a political agenda—while encouraging His followers to do the same.

The political version is friendly but quite polarizing, perhaps more polarizing than friendly. If you are not consumed with politics or the political process, His followers will be quick to shake their heads in disappointment, saddened that you are failing to carry out your purpose as a Christian. One undeniable characteristic of Political Jesus's followers is that they are persistent. They have a way of weaving all things political into every conversation, gathering, and prayer. Anyone who does not align with their political plans and desires are labeled as *too* something: too passive, too apathetic, too uninformed.

Political Jesus believes that cultural and moral change is accomplished through power and leverage, as opposed to grace and love. Therefore, Political Jesus's followers believe that the road to being a Christian nation is paved with legislation, and if you don't agree, get out of the way.

Fundamentalist Jesus

Quite simply, Fundamentalist Jesus is not nice and certainly not gracious. To His followers, the Bible is a source of truth but also a hammer used to beat people down. Followers of Fundamentalist Jesus say they are serious about righteousness, but all indications suggest they are more concerned with being *right*. Fundamentalist Jesus and His followers focus more on external behavior than internal character, because it is more measurable and easier to measure up to.

Fundamentalist Jesus can be seen showing up at parades, rallies, and street corners, often carrying a sign with a harsh message scrawled on it. The message often includes words such as *hates, despises,* or *condemns,* and will often connect those words with how God thinks about certain people, regardless of who the people may be. Fundamentalist Jesus draws a tight boundary on grace, which not only excludes those who do not follow Him but also excludes many who claim they do. Fundamentalist Jesus is quick to remind us that "the road is narrow that leads to life"—narrower than you may think. Walking the narrow road is not merely about placing one's trust in Jesus as Lord and Savior but also about dressing, worshipping, and behaving in compliance with an arbitrary list of standards. If not, "wide is the road that leads to destruction." Because Fundamentalist Jesus is this way, so are His followers. They view themselves as guardians of the standards list and protectors of the grace boundary.

Emergent Jesus

You know Emergent Jesus—He is hip and casual, and He has grown beyond "doing" church in any fashion that has been done before. There is an entire language He uses instead of terms that have been used by other Christians. You won't hear Him refer to a "worship service"; He prefers a "gathering" instead. He would not dare mention the teaching shared in the gathering as a "sermon," because it is a "lesson."

Emergent Jesus is friendly and cool. He is accepting of almost everyone, at least everyone not part of a traditional church setting. Those "traditional Christians" will likely be the object, whether directly or indirectly, of rolling eyes and dismissive remarks. Emergent Jesus would say that traditional customs and expressions of faith are old fashioned; being nontraditional is the way to go today. Emergent Jesus definitely has a knack for reaching new people, but sometimes at the cost of alienating most everyone else who also claims the name of Christ. Emergent Jesus comes dressed in torn jeans and an untucked plaid shirt, His arms decorated with a couple of tattoos (simply because He can), and perhaps with a beer in hand. And why not? As Emergent Jesus is quick to point out, there is freedom in Christ.

Mr. Rogers Jesus

One thing is for sure about Mr. Rogers Jesus—He would be a great neighbor. He is nice, safe, predictable, easygoing, gentle, and patient. Mr. Rogers Jesus never has to be told to use His inside voice, because that's the only kind of voice He has. He always talks in general terms, careful not to offend. He blushes at sin but isn't willing to do anything about it.

He is always around, but He is hesitant to give orders or direction. He prefers to stay in the background, avoiding any kind of controversy or adversity. He would prefer to remain the neutral neighbor everyone likes. In a pinch, Mr. Rogers Jesus is there at your beck and call, but if you need Him to keep His distance for the evening, just pull the blinds and He will oblige.

Obviously these profiles are exaggerated caricatures, and intentionally so. This list is certainly not exhaustive, because many other Build-A-Jesus variations exist. Of course, there are also hybrid versions that mix and match these profiles and others. The point here is to acknowledge that there is a Jesus identity crisis.

But He is not having the crisis. We are.

MISTAKEN IDENTITY

Many years ago, the famous silent-screen star Charlie Chaplin secretly entered a Charlie Chaplin look-alike contest. And he did not win. Seriously. A group of well-intentioned people determined that someone looked and acted more like Charlie Chaplin than the actual Charlie Chaplin.

A similar story could be told about Jesus, who is not some figment of a screenwriter's imagination. There is a real Jesus. However, if He showed up walking the streets of my city or yours, we might not recognize Him as Jesus. I know how uncomfortable that sounds. If you are like me, your defense mechanisms are shifting into gear and you are thinking, *Of course I would recognize Jesus. I have worshipped Him my whole life. I sing songs about Jesus. I know verses about Jesus. I even have a picture of Jesus hanging on the wall of my home.*

Trust me, I know the struggle. I am quick to say I would recognize Jesus too. But honestly, I'm not sure I would. Perhaps we would be more likely to label Him as a poser or an impostor, because in some ways He would not match up with our imagined Jesus. Maybe He would be more conservative or more liberal than your Jesus. He might be more or less dogmatic about doctrine than my Jesus. He might also take grace more or less seriously. He might place more emphasis or less emphasis on Sunday worship. He might cry more or less—or cry at different things—than your Jesus or mine.

There would likely be some serious differences between our Jesuses and Real Jesus, because our Jesuses are reflections of us. Our Jesuses are built within our hearts and minds, according to our preferences and desires. So when we study Scripture and read Jesus's teaching, we usually nod our heads in agreement, because we assume He is always talking to someone else.

I know I do that. I find myself thinking, *Way to go, Jesus!* Or, *Let 'em have it, Jesus!* Or, *You hit them right between the eyes with that line, Jesus!* Do you think those thoughts too? That question may be difficult to answer, so let me ask it in a different way. In many versions of the Bible, the words Jesus spoke are printed in red ink. When you read the red words, how do you usually feel? Encouraged? Convicted? Inspired? Perhaps the more pressing question is, when you read the red words, do you feel anything at all? The uncomfortable answer just might be no. The words may go in one ear and out the other. Or maybe you spend time contemplating what exactly Jesus meant, but even then there's not much feeling. If you find that you can read through pages of red letters without your heart racing, your palms sweating, and your mind spinning, there is a distinct possibility you don't understand whom Jesus is talking to.

He's talking to you. And me.

FILTERING JESUS'S WORDS

Deep inside our brains is the reticular activating system (RAS). All day, every day, everyone, everywhere, is being bombarded with millions and millions of stimuli. Sights, sounds, smells, sensations. If our minds tried to process and respond to all the stimuli, all the time, our brains would shut down because of overactivity. However, our brains don't even try to process and respond to all of it. That's because the RAS serves as a filter that determines what stimuli will be processed. There is one significant determining factor the RAS uses to determine which stimuli are allowed to pass into the brain: whether or not the stimuli are somehow relevant to you. If they are, the stimuli get in; if not, they don't.

This could just be my imagination running wild, but I wonder if the reason we can so casually read Jesus's words is because only some of the words are actually being processed by our minds. The other words and their implications are filtered out because they don't seem relevant to the Jesus we worship and serve. So when reading through Jesus's words—some of which should cause us to break out in a cold sweat and pace the floor—we can simply do so while curled up on a couch, humming our favorite song and sipping coffee.

In my experience, there is another tendency when studying Jesus's words: concluding that Jesus didn't mean exactly what He said. Have you heard those sermons? Read those books? Had those thoughts? A section of red letters is read and then is followed up with an interpretation of His real intent. Translation: these are Jesus's recorded words, but that's not really what He meant. There are several passages where this commonly takes place, but none more often than with the story called "The Rich Young Ruler" (Luke 18:18–23). We read that a person of power comes to Jesus inquiring about salvation. Based on the words used to describe him—*rich, young, ruler*—it would seem as though life was going really well for him. Yet he was clearly struggling with big questions, so he asked Jesus how he could gain eternal life. Jesus listed several commandments, and the young ruler assured Jesus that he had kept all of them since he was a boy.

I envision the young man holding his chin high with his chest puffed out, fully expecting Jesus to be impressed and to immediately grant him salvation. Instead, Jesus said, "You still lack one thing. Sell everything you have and give to the poor, and you will have treasure in heaven. Then come, follow me." The man walked away sad.

If this were a sermon you were listening to, you might hear the teacher explain how this story isn't about needing to eliminate wealth before being ready to follow Jesus well. So point one would be that Jesus didn't mean what He said, and the remainder of the sermon would explain what Jesus really meant.

I am a preacher, and I admit I have done this very thing. Even right now I am rationalizing in my mind how this passage really isn't about selling possessions as a great starting place to follow Jesus. You may find yourself doing the same.

Your Jesus would never demand such a thing. Neither would mine. We want Jesus's words, message, and instructions to fit within the framework of the Savior we envision Him to be. We don't want to deal with the incongruity of our *perception* of Jesus coming up against the *reality* of who He is. But the fact remains, to be like Jesus, we must be willing to acknowledge that our concepts of Him may not be accurate and then go in search of the truth.

Many have settled for Counterfeit Jesus, a Jesus who is content to imitate instead of be imitated. Have you?

3
COUNTERFEIT

Counterfeiting is a multibillion-dollar-a-year industry both domestically and abroad. It is a moneymaking industry. Literally. The success of counterfeit money completely depends on one factor: Does it look like the real thing? If it does, the money gets spent, saved, invested, and bartered with, as if it were the real thing. Only the most trained eyes can detect counterfeit money, and sometimes even the experts are fooled. Then the phony currency gets accepted into the monetary system as legitimate.

I suppose this is how and why counterfeit Jesuses are so often accepted, served, worshipped, and shared. By you, by me, and by so many others. He has the beard. He wears a robe. He has the smile on His face. He wants good things to happen in your life. He goes by the same name and, in our minds, looks like the real thing.

The question with counterfeit money is, how can you know it's fake? Criminologists who specialize in currency would tell you they do not learn to recognize counterfeit money by studying counterfeit money. Interestingly, they learn to recognize counterfeit money by studying real money. They become so familiar with the look, color, and feel of real money that when they lay their eyes on anything other than real money, they can usually recognize it. There is much more at stake with Counterfeit Jesus, but the question remains the same—how can you know? More specifically, how can you know if you have been worshipping, serving, sharing, or toting around a counterfeit Jesus?

This is a scary, uncomfortable question, but a necessary one. I am on this journey with you and am equally uneasy with this question. However, as I have spent time evaluating my life and faith, I have discovered that pondering a few other questions will help provide an answer.

1. Is your Jesus content to avoid certain areas of your life?

Take inventory of your life and determine if your Jesus stays away from one or more particular areas. For instance, perhaps Jesus leaves your finances alone. You have worn the *Christian* label for years, maybe even decades, and yet your year-end financial statements reflect zero money being invested in God's work on earth. No giving to your local church, parachurch organizations, or justice projects. Your Jesus is fine with that reality, because you are so generous in other areas of your life, such as time, energy, and talents.

It could be that your Jesus stays out of your romantic relation-ships. You are in a season of life in which you are trying to discover who would be the best life mate. Therefore, you wine and dine on a regular basis. Sometimes relationships develop; other times they don't. However, in many cases there is sexual involvement. You justify this by saying that you need to know if there's sexual compatibility or not. On Saturday night, your Jesus looks the other way, but on Sunday morning, your Jesus smiles as you walk into the local church. You have placed a Do Not Disturb door hanger on that area of your life, and your Jesus respects that wish.

Perhaps your Jesus steers clear of your professional life. In your workplace, you often hear, "The bottom line is the bottom line." Therefore, whatever behaviors positively affect the bottom line are not only accepted but also expected. Numbers are changed. Loopholes are found. Backs are stabbed. In many ways, your workplace is not an environment you would be comfortable having Jesus involved with, and so He gives you your space. On weekends, especially Sunday mornings, the two of you seem inseparable, but during the week some distance is necessary. Your Jesus understands, because you have to provide for your family.

The list of possible areas of life your Jesus avoids could go on and on. Whatever the situation, perhaps there is an area of your life that your Jesus avoids.

2. Is your Jesus content to leave you the way you are?

Understand, I am not asking, "Does your Jesus love you the way you are?" Because He certainly does. For years, the great evangelist Billy Graham chose the hymn "Just as I Am" to be played during his crusades as people responded to Christ. Appropriately so. Jesus loves you the way you are, but is your Jesus content to leave you the way you are? That is a completely different question.

A phrase is occasionally used in our culture to explain or justify a person's behavior. "Oh, that's just Charlie being Charlie." (Insert any name you want.) Maybe you have said that about someone you know, or maybe someone you know has often said that about you. The phrase is often playfully employed, but at its core, that statement is an excuse for bad behavior. Perhaps that line is used in reference to inappropriate humor, crude language, or a grumpy demeanor. With this phrase, the behavior is explained away. So in regard to less-than-righteous areas of your life, your Jesus is inclined to say, "Oh, that is just _____ being _____."

3. Is your Jesus leading you down a path that is only comfortable and safe?

I was tempted to remove this question from the list, and that temptation confirmed it needed to stay. This one hit a little too close to home, because I prefer my life and my path to stay comfortable. Do you? Does your Jesus cater to that desire? When you say Jesus is leading you to a new job, is it always one that pays better? When you say Jesus is leading you to buy another home, is it always larger, nicer, and more expensive? When you sense Jesus leading you into a new relationship, is it always with someone more physically attractive?

Another way to evaluate this question is by thinking in terms of risk. As you look at the path your Jesus is leading you down, how would you measure the potential discomforts and even dangers? Is He leading you out of your comfort zone or letting you stay there indefinitely? If your safety and security are the top priorities, you may want to examine your perception of Jesus.

4. Does your Jesus wink at sin?

As you think about the Jesus you know and serve, does He shout about grace but whisper about sin? Or perhaps just wink at sin? This question can be answered more accurately if you think honestly and specifically about sin that is present in your life. Gossip. Gluttony. Pornography. Jealousy. Self-righteousness. Pride. Greed.

A helpful way to determine how your Jesus responds to such sin is by honestly answering how *you* feel about such sin. If and when you repeatedly choose sinful behaviors, are you left with a knot in your stomach? A lump in your throat? Tears in your eyes? If so, the Jesus you know and love probably takes sin quite seriously. If not, your Jesus probably just winks at sin. And you probably do too.

5. If He were here on earth again, would your Jesus gravitate to the religious crowd?

Strange question, I know. But think about the Jesus you hold near and dear to your heart. If He were on earth in the flesh again, where would you most expect to encounter Him? Doing an evangelistic stadium tour? Touring elite seminary institutions? Visiting the Vatican? Or … walking in a shady, red-light district? Sleeping in a homeless shelter? Sitting on a stool at the local bar? Paying a visit to the county jail?

You can include any examples you want, but the important issue is determining with whom your Jesus would spend His time—with the religious crowd or with outcasts?

*

If you answered yes to any or all of these questions, then you have, at some level, settled for Counterfeit Jesus. I mean you are settling for a version of Jesus that is something other than Real Jesus. This behavior is nothing new, and the consequences are real and they are serious.

REALITY CHECK

Toward the end of His Sermon on the Mount, Jesus spoke some hard words:

> Not everyone who says to me, "Lord, Lord," will enter the kingdom of heaven, but only the one who does the will of my Father who is in heaven. Many will say to me on that day, "Lord, Lord, did we not prophesy in your name and in your name drive out demons and in your name perform many miracles?" Then I will tell them plainly, "I never knew you. Away from me, you evildoers!" (Matt. 7:21–23)

The temptation when studying this passage is to begin thinking sympathetically about all those *other* people Jesus is talking about. He must have been referring to people of another religious movement, the televangelist who experienced a moral failure, the coworker who doesn't interpret certain passages the way you do. But here is the thing: you might be one of the people He is talking about and the same is true about me. At the very least, these words from Real Jesus should cause us to pause and ponder about the Lord we know and serve.

The other temptation with this passage is to assume that Jesus is talking about people who never claimed to serve and know Him. But that's not reality. Did you hear the way the people responded? They immediately pointed to the good works they had done, the miracles they had performed, even the demons they had driven out. These are legit, card-holding followers of Jesus. Or so they thought. They may have been following *a* Jesus, but not Real Jesus. Perhaps they were followers of Counterfeit Jesus. They shaped their lives accordingly, and in the end Real Jesus essentially said, "You are out. You did not do My Father's will." This is not some fictional moment in time Jesus is talking about; He is pointing forward to the day of judgment. On that day, there will be some, perhaps even many, who show up to the judgment seat feeling confident, fully expecting to be granted a heavenly reward, only to be turned away.

These are cautionary words from Jesus. When He originally made these statements during the Sermon on the Mount, His listeners would have walked away understanding what was at stake—eternity. We would be wise to do the same. Don't be mistaken; God is not a mean-spirited schoolmaster, waiting to inflict punishment. But clearly there is a certain lifestyle that measures up to His will and desire. To end up disappointed on that day, spend your life following a counterfeit Jesus, a Jesus you have built your way, a Jesus who fits nicely into your life and comfort zone.

I hope this passage gets through your reticular activating system and you haven't already filtered it out, either consciously or subconsciously. If you immediately determine *other* people are going to end up disappointed, but don't give a thought to the possibility you may be part of that group, then you just might end up quite disappointed.

Even if the Matthew 7 passage were about other people, it should cause you a great deal of discomfort. As a pastor, I am devastated by the thought that some of the people I teach week after week, year after year, might be left out of heaven. They know the songs. They wear the T-shirts. They come to church regularly. On the outside, they have the appearance of being real, but in the end, some will be turned away with the words "I never knew you." These are disconcerting thoughts to entertain, let alone accept. But according to Real Jesus, they are true. When people settle for a counterfeit Jesus, they become a counterfeit Christian. They may fool some, they may even fool many, but Real Jesus will not be fooled.

REST ASSURED

Some people respond to this kind of uncomfortable truth by developing a sense of spiritual paranoia. When people experience this condition, they worry about whether they are saved or not saved, whether they are in the kingdom or out of the kingdom. This kind of paranoia is not from God and not of God. The Bible says we have an enemy who prowls around like a roaring lion looking for someone to devour. Our enemy is real. He is dangerous. And he is devious. One of his favorite tactics is causing people to question their salvation. I often meet with people who express these doubts. One day they feel certain they are living within the love and grace of God; the next day they feel just the opposite. This existence grieves God, who is a God of peace, but Satan finds great delight in it, because he comes to steal, kill, and destroy. Though at times people act as if these feelings are beyond their control, there is no benefit in living in a spiritual paranoia, afraid of what the verdict will be when judgment comes. So in response to Matthew 7, living in fear and paranoia is of no benefit. Instead, a helpful response is to do some honest evaluation.

Perhaps as you pondered the previous questions, you got a knot in your stomach or a lump in your throat. Perhaps that is God nudging you to wake up, look up, and listen up. If you have settled for a counterfeit version of Jesus, surely you didn't do so intentionally. However, you do need to be intentional with the next step—rebuilding.

Part II

IDENTIFICATION

4
REBUILDING

Rebuilding is no fun. My two boys are in the Lego stage, and we have been traveling this painful road for a while now. Painful? Have you stepped, full force, on a pointy Lego piece in the middle of the night? Enough said.

When playing with Legos, building is the fun part. With endless possibilities, your imagination can run wild. Instructions can be followed or unconstrained creativity can prevail. Legos can be moved and removed, placed and replaced. However, when my kids are playing Legos, inevitably the moment of weeping and gnashing of teeth comes (at least weeping). It doesn't happen during the construction phase; it happens during the deconstruction phase.

The deconstruction is not usually a gradual, methodical process—it usually occurs in one swift, sudden motion. Typically, kid brother comes in on a kamikaze mission and destroys what big brother worked so hard to build. Voices are raised. Angry words emerge. Tears flow. Then a rebuilding effort must be mounted.

Sometimes a similar event occurs with life-size materials. One summer, my uncle made the dubious decision to hire me to help build his mountain cabin. If placed in front of a lineup of tools, I could identify the hammer and saw, but that is where my expertise ends. But he asked and offered to pay well, so I agreed. One day, I was given the task of building a retaining wall that would line the driveway. The decorative stones had been delivered, the ground had been prepared, and the wall simply needed to be built. If only the task had actually been simple. With the hot sun overhead, I set to work. I placed one stone after the next, one layer after the next, until several hours later the retaining wall had been built. I was tired but proud. I stood there with arms crossed and a satisfied smile on my face as I beckoned my uncle to come and inspect my work.

As I watched his face fall and his eyes roll, I concluded something was not quite right with the wall. Perhaps the wall was taller than he had anticipated. Perhaps after analyzing my work, he realized he owed me more money than he had originally offered. But alas, that was not the case. Through clinched teeth, my uncle explained there was one slight problem with the wall—it had been built upside down. Oops.

Rebuilding is no fun, but it's often necessary.

DECONSTRUCTING THE COUNTERFEIT

If we have been following anything other than the true, authentic Jesus, we must set about deconstructing and reconstructing our images of Him. Counterfeit Jesus needs to be taken apart and properly put back together. What makes this process so difficult is that we built Him. You have built yours, and I have built mine.

Perhaps that is why imitating Jesus has never seemed to be much of a challenge. Your Jesus always agrees with you, and mine always agrees with me.

Everyone needs moments in their faith journey when they ask and answer hard questions. This is one of those times, and this is one of those questions: In your relationship with Jesus, who is doing the imitating? Jesus or you? Most of us are inclined to say we are the ones doing the imitating, because that's the way it's supposed to be. But often the opposite is true. His values just happen to match up with mine. His perspectives on finances just happen to align with mine. His doctrinal positions just happen to reflect my own. The reason you and Jesus rarely have difficult conversations and almost always agree is because He is imitating you instead of you imitating Him. All the while, Real Jesus resigns Himself to stand back and watch. He loves you and is fascinated by you, but will not spend one moment imitating you.

If you need to rebuild, where and how do you start? It begins with acknowledging reality. This sounds so simple, but it is uncomfortable nonetheless. Acknowledging that, at some level, you have built your own Jesus implies that He isn't necessarily going to act, think, talk, and live like you. Which means some radical changes might need to be made—not by Him but by you. Acknowledging you have built your own Jesus means that for a time, perhaps a long period of time, you have walked a path in vain. Perhaps the path you have walked veers from the one Real Jesus has called you to walk.

The path Jesus will call you to walk will likely be less comfortable, not as glamorous, and not as wide as the path you have been walking. Jesus said, "Small is the gate and narrow the road that leads to life" (Matt. 7:14). That statement contains many implications, but here is the pertinent one for our discussion: on a narrow road, we will not be walking side by side with Jesus but following in His footsteps.

As you might know or have possibly even experienced, Alcoholics Anonymous is a life-changing twelve-step recovery program. Step one centers around admitting that you have a problem—acknowledging your powerlessness over alcohol. The long journey of recovery begins by admitting the truth of the situation. Until this first step is taken, it will be impossible to take any of the subsequent steps.

Several years ago, I had the privilege of attending an AA meeting. I went because a friend of mine was celebrating his twenty-fifth year of sobriety. Because I had never been in that environment before, I soaked up every little detail of the experience. I found many aspects compelling, but none more so than the way people identified themselves. When people stood to speak, for any reason, they would first identify themselves this way: "Hi, I'm Bill, and I'm an alcoholic." Every person followed this same pattern, which I found fascinating and unsettling. I wondered why they would continue to identify themselves this way, always using a label and a not-so-flattering one at that. So I asked my friend, who explained and connected the dots for me. It all went back to the beginning, to the first of the twelve steps—acknowledgment and admission of the problem. I immediately understood. Without honest acknowledgment, there will be no recovery and no rebuilding.

Likewise, on our spiritual journey, rebuilding cannot occur without honest admission that we've been walking on the wrong path. We acknowledge the error of our ways so we can get back on track and start moving in the right direction—the direction Jesus has called us to. If you have built your Jesus, you have likely built your life and faith on the foundation of your Jesus.

BUILDING ON A FIRM FOUNDATION

Recall the Matthew 7 passage in which Jesus described how some will say, "Lord, Lord," and He will respond by saying, "I never knew you." In the very next breath, Jesus said,

> Therefore everyone who hears these words of mine and puts them into practice is like a wise man who built his house on the rock. The rain came down, the streams rose, and the winds blew and beat against that house; yet it did not fall, because it had its foundation on the rock. But everyone who hears these words of mine and does not put them into practice is like a foolish man who built his house on sand. The rain came down, the streams rose, and the winds blew and beat against that house, and it fell with a great crash. (vv. 24–27)

One day some houses are going to come crashing down. When those houses fall, they will not be rebuilt. It will be too late. Rebuilding can be done, but it must be done now. It's likely the thought of rebuilding is intimidating, even frightening. So much time, attention, and passion have been spent building a Jesus who looks and acts as you do.

After we've acknowledged the need for rebuilding, the next step takes us to the Gospels, where the words of Jesus appear and His deeds are recorded. For many of us, our images and understanding of Jesus have been shaped largely by well-meaning people in our lives: parents, grandparents, Sunday school teachers, camp speakers, television preachers. No matter who they are, it is likely your most fundamental impressions of Jesus stem from the words of several sincere, well-intentioned people. Perhaps the picture of Jesus they passed along was accurate, or perhaps not. It could be the understanding of Jesus they passed along aligns with one of the counterfeit Jesus profiles we already examined. Perhaps you have never even questioned the image of Jesus you have held dear. Whatever the case, we would do well to start with a clean slate, a cleared-off foundation.

In truth, none of us could ever really return to a completely clean slate and clear foundation. We all have presuppositions and worldviews that have shaped our thinking. So let's just agree to start with a *clean-ish* slate and *clear-ish* foundation. This brings us back to the gospels of Matthew, Mark, Luke, and John. Jesus is certainly mentioned in other places within the Scriptures. For instance, the Old Testament alone contains more than three hundred prophecies related to the life and death of Christ. Jesus is also mentioned and discussed in the New Testament epistles, as well as in the book of Revelation. However, nowhere is Jesus more readily accessible and observable than in the Gospels.

As we work to rebuild impressions of Jesus attribute by attribute, you may experience a wide array of emotions, including the temptation to return back to the Jesus you have always known—the Jesus you built. Resist the temptation. Though the journey of rebuilding

Jesus may be uncomfortable, inconvenient, and even frustrating, doing so is well worth it. Unless you identify Real Jesus, you cannot possibly imitate Real Jesus.

This struggle of mistaking who Jesus is and what He is like is nothing new. In fact, this Jesus identity crisis has been going on since the time He arrived on planet Earth. Prior to His coming, the Jewish religious leaders had been eagerly anticipating the arrival of a Messiah for generations. In the meantime, they conjured and conceived a Messiah within their hearts and minds. They had a specific image in mind of what He would look like, act like, and lead like. They had predetermined and precise expectations in mind for Him. So when the true Messiah came, they didn't recognize Him for who He was. They labeled Jesus an impostor and false teacher, and eventually murdered Him for claiming to be God. He was the Messiah. He just didn't match up with their picture of who and what the Messiah would be like.

Imagine if Jesus showed up again today. Would we treat Him the same way? I am sure you believe you would rush to His feet in worship or jump into His arms for a warm embrace or bow silently in adoration. I believe I would do the same. But perhaps you and I would actually label Him an impostor. If not, perhaps we would simply dismiss Him in favor of our own Jesus, because our Jesus is more comfortable, predictable, and familiar.

Real identification is healthy and necessary. Without real identification, there can be no real imitation.

5

HOLY ANGER

Several years ago, I found out about a new doll that was being sold. It was a not a Barbie doll, not a Ken doll; it was a Jesus doll. It was actually packaged and sold as a Jesus action figure and was advertised as the best action figure since G.I. Joe.

But wait, there's more. I have read that there is a new and improved version of the Jesus doll—and this one talks. The manufacturer advertises the toy as a "huggable, washable, and talking Jesus doll." He comes sporting fuzzy dreadlocks and a satiny beard, along with a string you can pull to get Him talking. He'll utter phrases such as, "I love you," "I have great plans for your life," and "Be good to your mother and father." All this for a bargain price of $15.95.

Frankly, the toy seems a bit silly to me, but if you or I designed the doll, I bet we would have it say similar phrases. These wouldn't be too difficult to come up with; after all, we expect to hear Jesus say certain things. None of us have seen Jesus, but all of us tend to have a picture in our minds of what He sounds like and looks like. Our images of Jesus would vary a bit, but the general picture of Him would probably be about the same. Flowing hair, big smile, sandals, white robe, blue sash—these elements are probably included in most of our mental images of Jesus. If we were to use words to describe our impression of Jesus, these would probably include *nice, kind, friendly*, and *polite*.

This sounds a lot like the Mr. Rogers Build-A-Jesus we discussed earlier, especially because the beloved television host was known for being gentle, warm, and affirming. Wonderful qualities, for sure, and I'm certain Jesus was these things too. But I'm also certain that Real Jesus was much more than the Mr. Nice Guy caricature so prevalent these days. If you study His story, you'll discover He said things that you wouldn't expect to hear coming from the Jesus doll. For instance, in Matthew 23, we find Jesus tangling with the legalistic religious leaders of the day. He tells them,

> You're hopeless, you religion scholars and Pharisees!
> Frauds! You burnish the surface of your cups and
> bowls so they sparkle in the sun, while the insides
> are maggoty with your greed and gluttony. Stupid
> Pharisee! Scour the insides, and then the gleaming
> surface will mean something. (vv. 25–26 MSG)

Whoa, that's not very Mr. Rogers–like. And other examples are just as scathing. What's more, you'll also find plenty of instances during which Jesus did things that don't seem to match up with His mild-mannered image. One such incident occurred when Jesus entered Jerusalem for what would be the final time, often referred to as His triumphal entry. Most kings would have come riding into the city on a white stallion, but Jesus came riding on a borrowed donkey.

As unassuming as His choice of transportation may have been, many identified who He was.

As He entered the city, people spread their cloaks on the road and shouted, "Hosanna!" which means "save us now." Many of these people recognized Him as the Messiah, but He wasn't the kind of Messiah they had been hoping for. After realizing Jesus didn't match up with their expectations, they started turning on Him. Some of the very people who praised Him a few days earlier shouted, "Crucify Him!" This is what happened:

> On reaching Jerusalem, Jesus entered the temple courts and began driving out those who were buying and selling there. He overturned the tables of the money changers and the benches of those selling doves, and would not allow anyone to carry merchandise through the temple courts. And as he taught them, he said, "Is it not written: 'My house will be called a house of prayer for all nations'? But you have made it 'a den of robbers.'"
>
> The chief priests and the teachers of the law heard this and began looking for a way to kill him, for they feared him, because the whole crowd was amazed at his teaching. (Mark 11:15–18)

At first glance, it seems as though He was throwing a temper tantrum, but of course there's more to the story. Some teachers misinterpret this passage as an admonition against selling anything in churches. When I was growing up, the church our family attended staunchly opposed anything being sold in church, even if the money was for a ministry opportunity, because temple commerce angered Jesus. But that's not the point of Jesus's actions and words. When He walked into the temple, at least two things infuriated Him.

First, people were being distracted from worship and prayer. The first place Jesus would have gone when entering the temple was the Court of Gentiles, the only area non-Jews were allowed. This is where gentiles could pray, worship, and offer sacrifices. Jesus walked into an environment not conducive to worship, with vendors and money changers engaged in business. It might have seemed like a huge flea market or even the floor of the New York Stock Exchange. Amid all the noise and commotion, haggling and bargaining, the gentiles attempted to worship. The place designed to help people draw near to God was keeping people from God. That made Jesus mad.

Second, there was exploitation of people, especially the poor. We know it wasn't bake sales and lemonade stands set up in the temple. The vendors were primarily selling doves. That's because foreigners would travel from miles away in every direction to come and make sacrifices, which required doves. Some people would show up without a dove, needing to buy one. Other people would bring their own, and an inspector would check it for blemishes or defects. If the bird was deemed unsuitable, worshippers were required to buy one from a vendor. Greedy vendors would charge exorbitant prices, as much as ten times the typical value. So people coming to the temple with pure intentions were exploited.

Even worse was the exploitation of poor people. The people required to pray and sacrifice in the Court of Gentiles would have been considered second-class citizens at best; they lived on the bottom rungs of society. These individuals were easy prey for conniving vendors and money changers.

What about the money changers? The Jewish people were required to travel to the temple to pay their dues and give a tithe. When travelers came from distant locations, their money had to be exchanged for Jewish currency. It isn't hard to imagine how exploitation took place in the exchange of money. Even now, when I travel internationally and have to exchange money, I always have someone I trust observe the transaction to make sure I'm dealt with fairly. Not only do travelers get charged to exchange money, but there's also a chance of being shortchanged. This was the scenario inside the temple—a situation ripe for swindling people.

We know from Scripture that God has a soft spot for the oppressed and downtrodden, such as orphans, widows, and beggars. So when Jesus saw how such people were being mistreated in the temple, He became furious.

GO AHEAD—GET MAD

Does anything make you mad enough to do something about it in the name of Jesus? It's obvious that Jesus displayed righteous indignation in an angry outburst aimed at stopping injustice. So being like Jesus means getting angry at situations involving unfairness or inequality—and being moved to act. I'm not talking about getting riled up and feeling our blood boil; I'm talking about an outrage that prompts us to right a wrong, eliminate oppression, or loose the chains of injustice. Isaiah 58:6–7 says,

Is not this the kind of fasting I have chosen:
to loose the chains of injustice
    and untie the cords of the yoke,
to set the oppressed free
    and break every yoke?
Is it not to share your food with the hungry
    and to provide the poor wanderer with shelter—
when you see the naked, to clothe them,
    and not to turn away from your own flesh and blood?

The truth is, in the hectic pace of life in twenty-first-century America, many of us are simply in survival mode, trying to make it from one day to the next. Under these circumstances, it's all too easy to get mad about the wrong things. If we did an honest evaluation of our lives, we might just find the things that make us mad are self-centered issues instead of others-centered issues. We get mad when we are cut off in traffic, don't get a raise, or receive an unexpected bill. I get mad at things such as these, just as most people do. But as imitators of Jesus, we should find ourselves getting angry over much larger, much more significant issues.

So what really makes you mad? I encourage you to take an honest inventory of the things you notice making you mad, because what causes our hearts to pound, our fists to clinch, and our voices to rise is an indication of our spiritual condition. Jesus was mad at the oppression that took place in the temple, so can you imagine how He must feel when He observes our world today? Men, women, and children are exploited and abused every day—not just in some faraway country but also in your community. As followers of Jesus, we have the responsibility to do what we can to release the oppressed people of this world. Maybe that means adopting an orphaned child, mentoring underprivileged teens, assisting a widow in practical ways, or volunteering with a relief organization.

As imitators of Jesus, our emotions should mirror His. This emotional mirroring is not mechanical but a natural result of relationship with Him. We should laugh when He would laugh, cry when He would cry, celebrate when He would celebrate, and express joy when He would express joy. All these emotions are appropriate, but I cannot help but wonder if we are lacking a strong dose of holy anger. I believe more Christians need to get fired up and let that passion prompt action in our churches, small groups, and families. I am not suggesting we stand on city street corners with signs declaring whom God hates. Nor I am suggesting we shout, stomp our feet, and make spectacles of ourselves. And I'm certainly not suggesting we carry out violence under the guise of following Jesus.

Holy anger is not driven by a desire to judge or to get revenge but by a desire to love people and to set them free. Holy anger does not involve screaming about your rights but advocating for the rights of others. Holy anger is not about proving a point but proving that everyone has value. Holy anger is not about personal gain but about restoring personal dignity to others.

Holy anger comes in many forms and is expressed in multiples ways, but the result is always the same: action is taken in the name of Jesus to loosen chains of injustice, restore dignity, and rescue people.

For several years, my wife and I lived in a small town in southwest Florida. In our town, there was a notorious low-class strip club. (I suppose that was a redundant statement. Is there such thing as a high-class strip club?) Some ladies in our church became burdened by the idea that countless young women were being oppressed in that place. Every evening as they stripped off their clothes, these young women were also being stripped of their dignity. They had become convinced that their worth and value were found in how they looked with their clothes off, but they needed to know that their real worth would be found being clothed in Christ. They believed that beauty was all about the outside; they needed to know that beauty is all about the inside.

The women from our church set their plan in motion to restore dignity to these young women who spent their evenings undressing in front of strangers. They had been told that many of these young women actually made very little money and likely struggled to meet their own practical needs, let alone the needs of their children. At the same time, we were doing a school-supplies drive at our church, so the women decided to use that as an opportunity to connect with some of the strippers.

One Friday afternoon, a few of the women from our church opened the doors to the club for the first time and entered that dark world. They asked the manager if there were any young women who needed practical assistance getting school supplies for their children. Surprisingly, the manager acknowledged there were several young women who could use the help. The next week the church women returned to the club with nice backpacks filled with every school supply a child would need, along with some special gifts to celebrate the start of a new school year.

While delivering the supplies, they were given the opportunity to meet a few of the girls, who wore bikinis by day and nothing by night. After a brief conversation, the church women learned that the girls rarely ate warm, home-cooked meals, and they expressed interest in being fed while working their evening shifts. So for the next several years, women of our church served the young ladies home-cooked meals, which they would place on a table in the dressing room backstage. As time passed and relationships developed, several of the ladies learned about the great love of Christ, and a few resigned from the club. Dignity was restored; some oppression was eliminated. Sometimes that happens when tables are turned over, other times when tables are set.

I think also of my dear friends Jeff and Brooke, who have taken seriously the call to care for orphaned children. After being told they would never have their own biological child, they set out on the journey to complete their first adoption. Ironically, during the process, Brooke became pregnant. Doesn't God have a sense of humor? During the last thirteen years, they have welcomed six children into their home, two biologically and four through adoption. Six children, two methods, all equally loved.

One of their children, Aaron, stands out in my mind. Born in China, he was brought into this world amid dire circumstances, with the extra challenge of suffering from albinism. This condition has no effect on his mind; it has merely dictated the shade of his skin. However, in China, a child born with albinism is considered to be second rate and an outcast. There is nothing that can change that cruel reality. Aaron was placed in an orphanage to wait his turn to be chosen. But who would choose a child who was deemed to be a mistake and doomed to a life of oppression and poverty? People like Jesus. People like my dear friends.

When Jeff and Brooke laid eyes on this boy for the first time, they knew he was meant to be theirs. So they began the expensive, intentional process of adoption and didn't stop until he was resting safely in their arms. Aaron has a million-dollar smile, beautiful skin, and a forever family, because my friends experienced a sense of holy anger and acted on it.

Jesus saw overlooked, "invisible" people clearly and gravitated to them quickly. So does Michelle, a well-educated, incredibly talented woman in the congregation I serve. For years, she committed her time and energy to raising her four children, but now that they are older she has been trying to identify where she will set her focus now. Michelle is an attorney, so common sense would suggest she should reenter the legal field, where she could command an impressive salary. Doing so would increase the financial security of her family, while also increasing her own visibility in tangible ways. Instead, she has chosen to focus on supposedly invisible people.

Michelle sensed a stirring to help refugees as they arrive and settle into our community. If anyone is supposedly invisible, it is refugees. They come from a place they no longer feel they belong, arriving at a place where they could easily feel the same way. They arrive not knowing the cultural customs, unable to speak the language, and incapable of navigating the societal systems on their own. Many people are too busy to even notice refugee families, let alone take the time to listen to and serve such families. Michelle is doing just that—listening and serving. Who knows exactly how God is using her to love refugee families, but it likely will not be glamorous. She will undoubtedly end up spending countless hours filing paperwork and dealing with bureaucracy. And she'll encounter frustrations and disappointments. The journey will not be prestigious, but action motivated by holy anger rarely is.

So what will it mean for you? What systems in your community need to be questioned? What rights need to be restored? What chains of injustice and oppression need to be loosened? Who needs to be spoken for and stood up for?

I don't have the answers for how to fix all that is broken, but I do believe sometimes we have to turn over tables in behalf of the oppressed and in the name of Jesus.

For some, it may feel uncomfortable to view Jesus as someone who became enraged and expressed His anger through physical action. But that is only because we so often settle for a false version of who Jesus was and how He behaved while on earth. Real Jesus is someone who, at least one time, walked into a temple and flipped tables upside down.

As you look around your community, do you find yourself experiencing holy anger that is resulting in action in behalf of the oppressed? If not, open your eyes. Start seeing Jesus in the oppressed, and the oppressed will start seeing Jesus in you.

6

REAL COMPASSION

I have seen Jesus.

I know how strange that sounds, but it's not exactly what it seems. Every now and then, we hear stories about people who claim to have seen the image of Jesus in their spaghetti noodles or a water stain. I remember hearing about a Missouri woman who was eating lunch and swore she saw the likeness of Jesus in one of her Cheetos. According to news reports, she keeps the prized Cheeto in her jewelry box. Let me just say it—that's weird. And it's not what I mean when I say I have seen Jesus, but I have definitely seen Him.

Several years ago, I was living and working in Louisville, Kentucky. It was a midsummer Saturday, with smothering heat and humidity. You could see the heat waves rising up off the asphalt. I had merged off the highway and coasted down to the end of the exit ramp. I waited patiently—or more likely, impatiently—for the light to turn green.

As I looked around the intersection, there he was. He was surprisingly tall—probably six foot four. He wasn't standing straight up, though, so it was hard to tell for sure. He wore tattered jeans, with holes that weren't a fashion statement. His shirt didn't fit well, but it seemed to be the least of his concerns.

The image of his face is still etched into my mind; I think it always will be. His beard was long and scraggly, partially covering wrinkled and sunbaked skin. The lines carved into his face and the bags under his eyes told his story for him.

As I studied him, we locked eyes. For a moment, I was tempted to look away, but I didn't—I just keep looking into his eyes. It has been said that the eyes are the windows to the soul, and if that is true, his soul was stained with rejection, broken promises, and shattered dignity. His hands, calloused and cracked, held a familiar sign: "Hungry. Homeless. Please help!"

A long line of cars waited at the light, and though most people did their best to ignore him, a few drivers held a hand out the window, offering change. As I watched the man begin to collect the change, I noticed he was disabled. One of his feet did not work properly, so he shuffled from car to car. The light turned green, and instead of turning left toward home, I turned right and pulled into a Perkins parking lot. I got out of my car and began walking in his direction. The closer I got to him, the more uncomfortable he looked. So instead of creating an awkward moment for him, I just waved my hand for him to come over to my car. When he arrived, looking a bit sheepish, I asked if I could have lunch with him. He agreed, and we began the journey to the McDonald's across the street. It should have been a quick jaunt, but with his disability, it was quite a challenge.

We finally got there, and after getting our food, we made our way to one of the outdoor tables so he could smoke while we ate.

At first, conversation was difficult. I think he felt awkward about the whole arrangement, and he seemed ashamed of his appearance. He told me his name was Mike, and he began to explain how his life had taken so many wrong turns. He showed me pictures of his niece, who was clearly his pride and joy. It was hard to follow his story down all the rabbit holes it took. But halfway through my second cheeseburger, I got the distinct impression that I wasn't just sharing a meal with Mike—I was sitting at an outdoor table in hundred-degree heat at a Louisville McDonald's, sharing fries with Jesus.

I have seen Jesus.

During the Christmas season one year, I was shopping at a local strip mall with my wife, Alex. Just when I thought we had finished, Alex informed me otherwise and began walking toward Michaels craft store, one of those huge places filled with wicker, candles, and ribbon—just the kind of store any guy would love. Years ago, I made a commitment not to enter such places, so when my wife went in, I courageously guarded the door outside.

After a few minutes, I saw a small woman walking down the sidewalk toward me. She was no more than five feet tall with very dark skin and was wearing tattered clothing, with her hair tucked beneath a knitted cap. Pushing a cart that probably contained all her worldly possessions, she seemed to be talking to no one in particular. As she got closer, I could tell that she was walking straight for me. I have never been afraid of a five-foot-tall woman before, but I started to get nervous because she looked angry with me. I glanced away, pretending I didn't see her, until she stopped her cart right in front of me and stared me up and down. Finally, she leaned close, opened her mouth, and nearly shouted, "How did you get so skinny? You need to put on some weight." Then she turned and walked away. I should have gone into Michaels with my wife.

In the following months, I continued to see that woman all over town. Sometimes she was sitting on the side of the road, eating a meal alone, other times fishing in a canal. Usually, she was just walking, but clearly she had a lot of needs—not just physical, but most likely emotional and spiritual as well. I didn't catch her name that night outside of Michaels, but I have a pretty good feeling it was Jesus.

I have seen Jesus.

When Alex and I were in the small coastal town of Port-de-Paix, Haiti, we spent a lot of time walking through the streets, meeting people. On one particular day, we were down by the beach, which is where some of the poorest of the poor live, and we saw an entire family sitting outside of their shack. With no jobs available, that is how they spent most of their days. When we got close, several children ran up to us, hoping we would give them something. We had been told not to hand out much food, but we wanted to give them the few granola bars we had with us.

Amid the noise and chaos, a particular child caught my eye. He was just a toddler. Flies were crawling all over his dark skin; tears had streaked his face. His belly protruded, a symptom of malnourishment. The roots of his hair were beginning to turn a burnt-orange color, another sign that hunger was ravaging his body. I had only one small box of raisins left, so we handed it to the boy's mother. I'm not sure if she gave it to him or not. It was one of those moments in life I will never forget. As I walked away, I realized that baby Jesus isn't always found lying in a manger.

I have seen Jesus.

JESUS IS EVERYWHERE WE CARE TO LOOK

In Matthew 25, Jesus tells a story that's often called the parable of the sheep and the goats. For a relatively short tale, it contains multilayered story lines. Mainly a glimpse of what judgment day will be like, it is also a challenge for His followers to treat everyone, especially the needy, as they would treat Him. This is what Jesus said:

> When the Son of Man comes in his glory, and all the angels with him, he will sit on his glorious throne. All the nations will be gathered before him, and he will separate the people one from another as a shepherd separates the sheep from the goats. He will put the sheep on his right and the goats on his left.
>
> Then the King will say to those on his right, "Come, you who are blessed by my Father; take your inheritance, the kingdom prepared for you

since the creation of the world. For I was hungry and you gave me something to eat, I was thirsty and you gave me something to drink, I was a stranger and you invited me in, I needed clothes and you clothed me, I was sick and you looked after me, I was in prison and you came to visit me."

Then the righteous will answer him, "Lord, when did we see you hungry and feed you, or thirsty and give you something to drink? When did we see you a stranger and invite you in, or needing clothes and clothe you? When did we see you sick or in prison and go to visit you?"

The King will reply, "Truly I tell you, whatever you did for one of the least of these brothers and sisters of mine, you did for me." (vv. 31–40)

So far it sounds as if judgment day will be a bed of roses. Perhaps it will for some, but certainly not for everyone. Jesus continues this way:

Then he will say to those on his left, "Depart from me, you who are crushed, into the eternal fire prepared for the devil and his angels. For I was hungry and you gave me nothing to eat, I was thirsty and you gave me nothing to drink, I was a stranger and you did not invite me in, I needed clothes and you did not clothe me, I was sick and in prison and you did not look after me."

They also will answer, "Lord, when did we see you hungry or thirsty or a stranger or needing clothes or sick or in prison, and did not help you?"

He will reply, "Truly I tell you, whatever you did not do for one of the least of these, you did not do for me."

Then they will go away to eternal punishment, but the righteous to eternal life. (vv. 40–46)

This passage is unique in that it seems to be the only picture of judgment day we are given in the New Testament. Judgment is mentioned or alluded to in other sections of Scripture, especially the book of Revelation, but according to my study, the only portrait of what that day might look like is Matthew 25. And the portrait is illuminating, if not surprising.

Most of us tend to believe that what will matter most on judgment day is religious achievement of some kind—church attendance, Scripture memorization, defense of the faith, accurate view of doctrine, number of people led to salvation, charitable organizations started, and so on. But if Matthew 25 is any indication, and I believe it is, one of the predominant factors will be compassion. That was *the* determining factor as Jesus separated the sheep from the goats. This comes as good news for most people, because most people consider themselves compassionate. Still, most of us do not have a solid understanding of what compassion really is.

Dictionary.com defines compassion as "a feeling of deep sympathy and sorrow for another who is stricken by misfortune, accompanied by a strong desire to alleviate the suffering." That is the way most of us view compassion, and so we categorize compassion as a feeling or a desire. According to that understanding, most of us would pass the test because we all experience that feeling. It appears in many different situations.

- Watching late-night television, you flip through the channels and stop when you see starving children on the screen. You realize it is one of those "Feed the Children" documentaries. You see the desperation in their eyes and the look of hunger on their faces, and your stomach ties up in knots. Soon, as you drift off to sleep, you feel profoundly compassionate.
- You are waiting in line at the grocery store. The young mother in front of you has two kids in the cart, one in her arms, and another on the way. With the kids crying for her attention and begging for a candy bar, she rustles through her food stamps. As she checks out and walks away, tears well up in your eyes as you are overwhelmed with the feeling of compassion.
- You have a neighbor kid who is overweight and awkward. He gets made fun of and picked on by the other kids. His parents are never around, and he sits alone on the porch much of the time. Probably a target of bullies at school, he has no friends that you've ever seen. Your heart goes out to him. You're filled with compassion for the poor kid.

You've probably picked up on the pattern. For most of us, compassion often begins and ends with a feeling. But not for Jesus. In fact, Jesus would likely say any feeling that doesn't lead to action should be called something else, not compassion. As you study Jesus's life in the Gospels, you will find that He redefined compassion. For Jesus, compassion never stopped with a feeling; it always led Him to act. For example:

> When Jesus landed and saw a large crowd, he had compassion on them and healed their sick. (Matt. 14:14)

> Jesus had compassion on them and touched their eyes. Immediately they received their sight and followed him. (Matt. 20:34)

> Jesus was indignant. He reached out his hand and touched the man. (Mark 1:41)

Jesus modeled what I call the "compassion and" principle. When situations arise that cause us to feel compassion, we should not let the experience stop there. These should be "compassion and" moments, with the "and" being actions that follow the feelings. Of course, we cannot meet every need, feed every starving child, fill every tank with gas, or befriend every lonely person. We can't do everything, but if we wear Christ's name, we must do *something*.

OVERCOMING THE OBSTACLES

As we begin to understand compassion as an action instead of a feeling, some of us will have to acknowledge that we have some growing to do in this area. When there is a lack of action, there is a lack of compassion. Interestingly, the obstacle that keeps many people from moving into action is one simple question—why? A "why" question often and easily slips into the back of our minds when we encounter compassion opportunities, and because there is never a good enough answer, it becomes an excuse to do nothing.

> Why doesn't he just get a job?
> Why doesn't she just take some initiative?
> Why do they expect everyone else to support them?
> Why does she keep having kids when she can't even
>   support the ones she has?
> Why does he continue smoking when he can barely
>   afford to eat?

Interestingly, none of those questions show up in Matthew 25, or anywhere else, during Jesus's earthly ministry. I know that a lot of times "why" questions are asked with pure motivations, because the last thing you want to do is to enable an addiction or encourage irresponsible behavior. Maybe it even feels as though asking these questions is the right thing to do because, after all, "God helps those who help themselves." Wrong. That's not actually a Bible verse, as so many think it is; plus it is contrary to the verses that are found in the Bible. The very story of grace is not that God helps those who help themselves, but that God helps those who cannot help themselves. When Jesus encountered opportunities to act with compassion, not one time did He ask a "why" question.

When Jesus met the woman at the well who had already been married several times and was then living with another man, He didn't ask why. He just introduced Himself and told her where she could find living water.

When Jesus met the lame, He didn't ask why. He just told them to walk.

When Jesus encountered the leper, He didn't ask why. He just said, "You are clean."

So when you begin to feel compassion, don't let it stop with asking why. Instead, let the feeling lead to action. When you stop at the feeling, you are not just missing out on an opportunity to serve a hungry child or a young mother or an outcast; you are missing out on a divine appointment with Jesus.

LOVE IN ACTION

Shortly after World War II came to a close, Europe began picking up the pieces. Much of the Old Country had been ravaged by war and was in ruins. Perhaps the saddest sight of all was that of orphaned children starving in the streets of those war-torn cities.

Early one chilly morning, an American soldier made his way back to the barracks in London. As he turned the corner in his Jeep, he spotted a little lad with his nose pressed to the window of a pastry shop. Inside, the baker was kneading dough for a fresh batch of doughnuts. The hungry boy stared in silence, watching every move. The soldier pulled his Jeep to a stop at the curb, got out, and walked quietly over to where the little fellow was standing.

Through the steamed-up window, the boy could see the mouth-watering morsels being pulled from the oven, piping hot. He salivated and released a slight groan as he watched the baker place them onto the glass-enclosed counter ever so carefully. The soldier's heart went out to the nameless orphan as he stood beside him.

"Son," the soldier finally said, "would you like some of those?"

Startled, the boy replied, "You bet I would!"

The American stepped inside, bought a dozen, put them in a bag, and walked back to where the lad was standing in the foggy cold of the London morning. He smiled, held out the bag, and said simply, "Here you go."

As the soldier turned to walk away, he felt a tug on his coat. He looked back and heard the child ask quietly, "Mister, are you Jesus?"

What a grand compliment to receive that question. I would be thrilled if someone saw just a trace of Jesus's love and compassion in my actions, and I bet you would too. People are not going to mistake us for Jesus because we show up at a church building on Sunday morning. However, they might mistake us for Jesus when we love in a way that doesn't make sense, when we give beyond what is expected, when we take risks that do not seem rational. We resemble Jesus the most in the midst of active compassion. Here are just a few practical ways to live out compassion:

- Set aside some money each month for gift cards to local restaurants. Keep them in your car, and when you see a homeless person, give out a card.

You will not only fill a stomach, but also, for one meal, restore dignity.

- Spend an afternoon at a nursing home, going from room to room to offer conversation and hugs. Nursing-home residents are often among the loneliest people in our society.

- Go into a Laundromat on a Saturday evening with a pocketful of quarters, and pay for loads of laundry to be done.

- Visit a group home for adults with disabilities to make sure they know they have not been forgotten.

- If there is a widow who lives in your neighborhood, spend an afternoon with your family taking care of her yard or doing a project in her home. It will be a gentle reminder that, though she may be lonely, she is not alone.

When we live out active compassion, people may catch a glimpse of Jesus, and they just might also hear His voice saying, "I love you." Jesus's active compassion did not just radically affect a few people here and there in Scripture; Jesus's active compassion has everything to do with you and me. He has shared His compassion with us and calls us to follow His example.

I have seen Jesus. I hope that someone will say the same after an encounter with me or with you.

7
MESSY LOVE

How would you complete the following sentence? Love is
_____.

Maybe you would use one of these words: *Blind. Wonderful. Necessary. Unconditional. Powerful. Frightening. Life changing. Beautiful. Risky. Eternal.*

Thousands of different words could be placed in that blank. I could fill up the pages of this book with various words that would make sense and seem appropriate. Given the opportunity, you could likely continue filling in that blank over and over until your hand developed a cramp and you were forced to put down the pen.

Similarly, you could walk the aisles of any card shop and find love described in endless ways. Some descriptions are inspiring, others are warm and fuzzy, and still others are pathetically sappy.

In his letter to the church of Corinth, the apostle Paul wrote what is often considered to be the greatest dissertation on love. He began by using the same pattern as the question I posed above. Love is _____. He then employed language and

descriptions that are considered among the most beautiful depic-
tions of love in all of literature, religious or otherwise. Here is a
sample:

> Love is patient, love is kind. It does not envy, it does
> not boast, it is not proud. It does not dishonor oth-
> ers, it is not self-seeking, it is not easily angered, it
> keeps no record of wrongs. Love does not delight in
> evil but rejoices with the truth. It always protects,
> always trusts, always hopes, always perseveres….
>
> And now these three remain: faith, hope and
> love. But the greatest of these is love. (1 Cor.
> 13:4–7, 13)

In 1 John 4:8, the author the reverses this approach to describing
love and, instead, provides the ultimate definition. "God is love."
God is not only love but also the Author and Creator of love and
therefore most equipped to describe exactly what it is. If we had the
opportunity to ask God how He would define love, I imagine that
He wouldn't use adjectives at all, preferring, instead, to offer a flesh-
and-blood example. I believe He might simply point to His Son,
Jesus, and say, "If you want to know what love looks like, then look
no further than the life and death of Jesus."

When you start following Jesus through the pages of the Gospels,
you quickly see that His way of loving people was unconditional,
sacrificial, and complete. He offered total love to the rich and poor,
the powerful and lowly, with no strings attached. Another important
lesson we learn as we look at Jesus's example: love is messy. Though

we often use beautiful language to describe love, when we put it into action in everyday life, it is often less than perfect and pristine.

The church I serve developed a mission statement several years ago, which says simply, "Love Jesus. Love like Jesus." These phrases look so great when printed on church stationery, banners, and plaques. They form a statement that is memorable and easy to repeat by people of all ages. It rolls right off the tongue. These short phrases may seem neat and tidy, safe and secure, but are quite the contrary when you think about what is involved in fulfilling the mission. In fact, I have been thinking that when we print that mission statement, we should, for the sake of full disclosure, put an asterisk after the phrase "Love like Jesus," with a footnote that says, "Caution: Love is messy."

JESUS LOVES MESSED-UP PEOPLE

There they stood—religious leaders, Jesus, and a woman. The woman was probably scantily clad, if she was clad at all. After all, she had been caught in the act. She met the man at the agreed upon time and place, not just to hang out but to hook up. And they did. Whether it was the first time or just *a* time, we don't know. But there they were, with sheets tussled, frolicking, fornicating.

Daytime, nighttime, we don't know. But they were having a time … and were no doubt shocked when time ran out. Caught red-handed and red-faced. It is certainly curious that religious leaders happened upon the two impassioned participants. It's even more curious that they took interest in punishing only the woman, while the man is never mentioned and nowhere to be found. Perhaps he grabbed his tunic and fled the scene. More likely, the religious leaders had an agenda.

So there she stood, probably clutching a sheet to hide her naked-ness, before Jesus. John 8 says the religious leaders took the woman to Jesus and asked Him to tell them what they should do with her. Aha! Their ultimate goal had not been to trap the woman but to trap Jesus. They knew, and Jesus knew, that according to Old Testament law, stoning was the appropriate and acceptable punishment for someone caught in adultery. As the showdown between Jesus and the religious leaders began, those in the crowd had already chosen rocks to throw, ready to mete out the ultimate penalty. Vengeance was on their minds, and they were prepared to have blood on their hands.

It would have been easier for Jesus to give the expected and desired answer—go with the letter of the law. Or He could have turned and walked away, choosing not to get involved in such a sordid affair. But He stayed, because He had come to love, and love is messy.

Without a word, He knelt down and began writing in the dirt. We are not told what He wrote, but there's been lots of speculation. Some suggest He wrote out a prayer. Perhaps He scribbled an Old Testament passage about God's mercy. Or He might have listed the names of the people in the crowd, along with the sins they had com-mitted. We can't know for sure what He scrawled in the dirt, but we do know the words that finally came out of His mouth.

With anticipation thick in the air, Jesus simply said, "Let any one of you who is without sin be the first to throw a stone at her."

Then, silence.

One by one, rocks moved through the air. Not racing toward the adulterous woman, but gently falling to the ground.

Then the crowd disappeared. What began as a large, angry mob had dwindled to two unlikely people: Jesus and the woman.

With the threat diverted because of His love, Jesus spoke truth to her in love. "Woman, where are they? Has no one condemned you? … Then neither do I condemn you…. Go now and leave your life of sin" (John 8:7–11).

You might be familiar with this story. Many scholars have debated the legitimacy of this passage, whether it should or shouldn't be included in Scripture. I don't know the answer to that question, but my fear is that in the midst of that debate, the love lesson gets lost. Love is costly, risky, and messy.

Oftentimes people set out to love like Jesus but think they will be able to do so from the safe, comfortable confines of the church pew or the living room recliner. Their intentions to love are good, but their expectations are way off. Jesus's brand of love usually isn't shared in safe, comfortable spaces but oftentimes amid problematic and painful circumstances. Sometimes the messiness of love will mean dirt under your fingernails, and sometimes the mess will wreck your schedule or preempt your weekend plans.

I confess I don't always handle interruptions well. I don't explode with anger, lash out at anyone, or mutter offensive words under my breath. On the outside, I usually remain composed, but on the inside, not so much. I think, *Don't you see I am busy here? Don't you realize I have a lot of work that needs to be done? Don't you know I have tons of important things to do?* Smiling on the outside, seething on the inside.

How do you handle interruptions? For many of us, the way we typically respond to being interrupted by people is to be annoyed, frustrated, angry, or perhaps sarcastic. Most of us consider interruptions to be inconvenient at best and intolerable at worst. We respond that way, but Jesus didn't. He knew that interruptions come with the territory of loving others. He not only accepted interruptions but also embraced them. Oftentimes when people tried to intrude on Jesus's activities, His disciples tried to intervene as the gatekeepers and guardians of the schedule. They shooed people away, thinking Jesus had better things to do. They urged little children to leave, and they told a begging blind man to quiet down. Every time, Jesus stopped the disciples and welcomed the people.

DIVINE INTERRUPTIONS

Here is what Jesus knew, what I am discovering, and what we all need to learn: you cannot schedule love. The difference between Jesus's perspective toward interruptions and ours is that we view interruptions as inconveniences; Jesus viewed interruptions as divine appointments to love.

When faced with disruptions to our plans and schedules, we might protest, "But I have lots of really important things to do." And Jesus would say, "So did I." We might insist, "But a lot of people depend on me." And Jesus would say, "Me too." We might claim, "Modern life is overwhelming. I'm too busy to deal with interruptions." And Jesus would say, "If you're too busy to love people, you might want to rethink your commitments." Any excuse we come up with to ignore interruptions, Jesus could have topped them. Yet over and over, Jesus embraced interruptions when they involved people, because Jesus loves people and never missed an opportunity to show it.

Early in the book of Mark, we read, "A few days later, when Jesus again entered Capernaum, the people heard that he had come home. They gathered in such large numbers that there was no room left, not even outside the door, and he preached the word to them" (2:1–2).

Jesus had no office, but you might say this was just another day at the office for Him. As you study His ministry, you find that large crowds of people constantly surrounded Him. Even when Jesus tried to escape for some silence and solitude, the people always found Him. And when people surrounded Him, He never missed an opportunity to teach them.

We shouldn't be surprised, then, to read in Mark 2 that Jesus was teaching to a standing-room-only crowd. In fact, we are told there was not even any room outside the door—people poured out to the front of the house and perhaps out on the street. This sets the stage for what happens next.

> Some men came, bringing to him a paralyzed man, carried by four of them. Since they could not get him to Jesus because of the crowd, they made an opening in the roof above Jesus by digging through it and then lowered the mat the man was lying on. (vv. 3–4)

Palestinian houses had flat roofs, with beams laid across and packed tightly with clay and brush. Because the roof often served as a place of rest, usually an outdoor stairway led to that area. It would not have taken much effort for these men to burrow a hole through the roof, which could have easily been repaired. They carried their paralyzed friend to the rooftop, dug a hole, and lowered the man down in front of Jesus.

This would qualify as an interruption, right? Imagine Jesus in the midst of teaching this large crowd of people, when suddenly He started hearing noises above His head. At first, He might not have thought much of it, because people often went on their rooftops. But then pieces of dirt and debris began falling on His head. Looking up, He saw a shaft of sunlight emerging through a hole. Surely the people in that room noticed what was going on. And surely the teaching paused as everyone waited to see what would happen next.

I imagine some of the audience members scooted to the edges of their seats, wondering how Jesus would respond. Here He was, a respected rabbi, with an important message to share, being rudely interrupted as a man lying on a mat was lowered down.

We don't know much about the paralyzed man except that he had great friends to make such an effort in his behalf. We also know that at the time there was no government assistance for disabled people and very few ways for someone in his condition to scratch out a living. Likely, he spent his days seated on the ground on a busy street, begging for meager handouts and a little loose change.

Perhaps while sitting by the streets, this man heard people talk about the rabbi Jesus, who was said to have healing powers. Desperate, he enlisted his friends to take him to a house meeting where the rabbi would teach. Not wanting to miss their chance, they decided to go for it. This disrupted Jesus's plans for a soul-stirring message about the kingdom of God, but I imagine He admired the ingenuity, audacity, and faith of the paralytic and his friends. So Jesus said, "I tell you, get up, take your mat and go home" (Mark 2:11). Astonished, the crowd parted as the man walked out of the house.

At some point, the members of the crowd also walked out of the house and returned back to their homes. I can imagine how their conversations went as they traveled their separate ways and recounted what they had seen. Some were likely appalled by the hole that was torn in a perfectly good roof. Others surely were perplexed about why Jesus didn't scold the men for vandalizing another person's house; instead, He rewarded their seemingly reckless behavior. But, specifically, I wonder how they would describe the whole experience if they were allowed only one word to do so. Hectic? Shocking? Irresponsible? Confusing? I don't know for sure, but I imagine words such as these and others would be used in a description of the day's events.

Hindsight is always 20/20, right? So looking back on that day, I can quite clearly describe the experience with just one word—*love*. Love happened. A sermon was postponed, a roof was destroyed, a religious crowd was offended … but love was extended and received. Love is costly and inconvenient, but most of all, love is messy.

We could look at numerous examples of times when Jesus demonstrated love amid messy circumstances. He touched lepers, laid hands on dead people, reached out to beggars, hung around prostitutes, dealt with demon-possessed individuals, let kids climb on Him, went without food, and got soaking wet. Messy love will at times mean discomfort; other times it will be mean an upended schedule; and at times it will be a matter of blood, sweat, and tears. Figuratively and sometimes literally.

It was a Friday afternoon. Jesus was tired. Bloodied. In custody. In chains. All throughout the previous evening, accusations had been made and charges filed, but there was no evidence to substantiate the claims. His innocence was undeniable, but for those involved, His innocence was also irrelevant. They wanted Him. Not dead or alive. Just dead.

While praying in the garden, He had been arrested. Next He was tried and beaten beyond recognition, then prodded and poked as He stumbled and crawled toward the hill just outside the city. Though despised and rejected, He had come to love. Already His love mission had been evidenced by the dirt under His fingernails and His constantly interrupted schedule, but that Friday His love would be found in His literal blood, sweat, and tears. There were a crown and a robe. Just what every king deserves, but there was no throne for Him to sit on. Instead, there was a cross on which He would lie and then hang.

When the spectacle was over, the crowd of onlookers would have walked away, returning to wherever they had come from. Along the way, there would have been conversations. Opinions would have been offered, perhaps voices raised, about what had just happened on the hill outside the city. Some people were probably certain; others were likely confused. *Murder. Justice. Vengeance.* These words and others would have been used to describe the day, but all would fall short of what had really taken place. Love. Love happened. For Jesus, love was a matter of life and death.

You will not likely be called to die in the name of love, but you are most definitely called to live in the name of love.

To join the fray of loving like Jesus loved requires a radical shift of heart and mind, as well as a practical shift in expectations and plans. Any hope of remaining safe, predictable, and clean must be traded for the expectation of uncertainty, instability, and perhaps danger. The path of love we are called to walk is not a broad road with clear markings, devoid of any potholes or pitfalls; it is a narrow road, a road splattered with mud and sometimes blood. I know it sounds a bit messy, but love always is.

8

SIMPLE OBEDIENCE

When I was growing up, I was taught quite adamantly to avoid using any kind of four-letter word. Words such as %&*# and @$*&, not to mention !$@^. There was no acceptable excuse to use or associate myself with such language. So as the compliant kid that I was, I stayed far away from all four-letter words.

Maybe this explains why I struggled a bit with obedience. At some point along the way I realized that the shortened version of *obedience—obey—*is a four-letter word.

Several years ago I attended a leadership retreat, and each participant had been asked to take a personality test ahead of time. Then during the retreat, we met individually with a facilitator who helped us better understand our personalities, based on the test results. One of the areas the test evaluated was compliance. In other words, how readily do you color within the lines, how easily do you conform, and how willing are you to follow rules? Let me just say, certain aspects of the personality test revealed admirable characteristics about me ... and then there was the compliance section. I scored a zero in the area of compliance. I am not convinced those results were really accurate, though, because I never read the test instructions.

Unlike me, plenty of people score high in the area of compliance. Maybe you're one of them. You are eager to follow rules, love to color inside the lines, appreciate a list of instructions (and actually read them), and would never dream of going through the fifteen-item express lane at the grocery store with sixteen items in your cart.

But the truth is, most people, no matter their personality type, do not get enthused and energized by discussing obedience. In our culture, obedience is not a characteristic held in high esteem. Every year, *People* magazine publishes its "50 Most Beautiful People" issue, and *Forbes* has its "100 Wealthiest People" edition. But I have yet to see a magazine come out with a "50 Most Obedient People" issue, and if any did, it wouldn't be flying off the racks. Magazine covers are not usually graced with Mr. or Mrs. Moral Compliance. Instead, covers are splashed with pictures of people embroiled in affairs, scandals, addictions, or criminal activities. In other words, noncompliant types.

Even though our society does not encourage or applaud it, obedience must be taken seriously if you want to imitate Jesus. That's because He took obedience seriously. When considering Jesus's obedience, we tend to think it was easy for Him because He was sinless. After all, He was God. But hold on. The book of Philippians tells us that while He was fully God, He was also fully flesh-and-blood human.

> Who [Jesus], being in very nature God, did not
> consider equality with God something to be
> used to his own advantage;

> rather, he made himself nothing
>> by taking the very nature of a servant,
>> being made in human likeness. (Phil. 2:6–7)

The writer of Hebrews puts it this way in chapter 4:

> For we do not have a high priest who is unable to empathize with our weaknesses, but we have one who has been tempted in every way, just as we are—yet he did not sin. (v. 15)

In the beginning of His ministry, Jesus spent forty days fasting and praying in the desert. While Jesus was there, Satan began to tempt Him, trying desperately to lure Him into disobedience. Satan isn't wise, but he is also not stupid. And he knew that if he could get Jesus to settle for something less than God's plan, for even a moment, then the entire work of salvation would be crushed before it got started. So Satan did what he often does—he met Jesus in the midst of his weakness, fatigue, and hunger. "After fasting forty days and forty nights, he was hungry. The tempter came to him and said, 'If you are the Son of God, tell these stones to become bread'" (Matt. 4:2–3).

Satan wasn't asking Jesus to commit moral suicide of some kind; he simply tempted Him to eat. Jesus could easily have turned the stones into bread. This is the same person who would later multiply a few fish and loaves of bread to feed a crowd of thousands, the same man who told the wind and the waves to calm down and they did, the same man who cast out demons, and the same man who turned water into wine.

So why didn't He just turn the stones into bread? What was the big deal? That question is often the very one we ask about disobedience to God. The question gets played out like this:

- "No, we're not married, and yes, we are living as though we're married. But it works for us and no one is getting hurt, so what's the big deal?"
- "I indulge in pornography, but at least I am not actually going out and having an affair on my spouse. And I do it when no one else is around, so what's the big deal?"
- "A few numbers get changed here and there at work to make the bottom line look better. But I'm pressured by my boss to do it. Besides, the government gets too much of the profit anyway, so what's the big deal?"

The question goes a lot of different ways, but it gets asked about sin all the time: What's the big deal? The best answer comes from the example of Jesus, who responded by saying, "It is written: 'Man shall not live on bread alone, but on every word that comes from the mouth of God'" (Matt. 4:4). In other words, the purposes of God are more important than the desires of people; the will of the Father trumps the wishes of people.

Satan tried another approach. He took Jesus to a high place and tempted Him to jump, saying that if He were really the Son of God, He could make the leap and not get hurt. Satan even quoted Scripture to up the ante. "For it is written: 'He will command his angels concerning you, and they will lift you up in their hands, so that you will not strike your foot against a stone'" (v. 6).

Jesus again refused to cave in, quoting Scripture right back: "It is also written; 'Do not put the Lord your God to the test'" (v. 7).

Not one to give up easily, Satan tempted Jesus one more time. "Again, the devil took him to a very high mountain and showed him all the kingdoms of the world and their splendor. 'All this I will give you,' he said, 'if you will bow down and worship me'" (vv. 8–9).

Jesus didn't take the bait. He said, "Away from me, Satan! For it is written: 'Worship the Lord your God, and serve him only'" (v. 10).

Each time Jesus was tempted by Satan, He responded with Scripture. Likewise, for you and me, having our hearts and minds filled with Scripture will always be the best way to resist temptation. Moreover, Jesus didn't come to fulfill the request of any person or pursue a personal agenda; He came to fulfill His Father's will. When you are living primarily to do God's will, you are empowered to stay focused on eternal purposes and not succumb to temporary ambitions.

MORE THAN RIGHT VERSUS WRONG

The reason for obedience is pretty simple: sin of any size, shape, or kind diverts us from our mission of fulfilling God's will. Sin is more than doing things God says not to do; it is also failing to do what He calls us to do. I believe God's will isn't primarily about "thou shalt nots," but "thou shalls." It's about doing the *right* thing, not just avoiding the *wrong* thing.

So the question must be asked, what is God's will? Most Christians would say, "If I just knew God's will for my life, I would do it." Typically, when people talk about God's will, they are usually interested in learning specific details. Where does God want me to go to college? What career path does God want me to choose? Who does God want me to marry? Where does God want me to live? All in the name of wanting to know God's will for their lives, people lose sleep, experience stress, and worry endlessly.

What happens all too often is that people get hung up on trying to discover God's specific will for their lives and overlook the importance of living out His general will. When I refer to God's general will, I mean the truths, instructions, and commands that apply to everyone. Love, compassion, forgiveness, generosity, humility—these are attitudes and actions that every follower of Jesus should strive to live out. God's specific will pertains to truths, instructions, and commands that apply specifically to *your* life. God might be calling you to a particular vocation that would use your talents and bring you joy. He might be directing you to a certain ministry opportunity where your unique abilities would be put to good use.

Consider a few examples of people focused on finding God's specific will, while forgetting to follow His general will:

- A young, single man who desperately wants to know whether or not God is calling him into full-time ministry, all the while being intimately involved with his girlfriend.
- A professional woman who is praying about which career opportunity she should pursue next

and, in the meantime, refusing to be generous with God or others.

- The husband and wife who wonder which country God would have them adopt from, but also spend most weekends partying hard and getting drunk with friends.

There is a principle we need to weave into our lives. Instead of becoming consumed with the uncertainties of God's specific will, let's first and foremost be committed to fulfilling the certainties of God's general will.

THE HEART OF OBEDIENCE

Jesus seemed to raise the bar high for His disciples when He declared, "If you love me, keep my commands" (John 14:15). That statement would be much easier to swallow if there were room for interpretation. In this statement Jesus didn't leave room for interpretation. It's clear-cut: the best indication of our love for Him is our willingness to obey Him.

We are not called to be perfect, and God always extends grace when we fall short. We can never *earn* God's love by being good, and we can never *lose* His love by being *bad*. Jesus, I believe, is saying that if we truly love Him, we will take seriously all the guidelines He has laid out for godly living, and we will do our very best to follow them. Undoubtedly, moral compliance has been chosen many times in hopes of impressing Jesus, but that is not the proper motivation. The proper motivation is love. If you love Jesus, you obey Him.

How do you suppose Jesus would evaluate your obedience to—and therefore your love for—Him? You may expect Him to ask questions such as these:

1. Have you been drunk in the last thirty days? How many times?

2. Do you look at pornographic material?

3. Are you enjoying television shows that should really cause you to cringe (or weep)?

4. Do you spread gossip and rumors?

5. Are you completely honest in the area of your finances?

Those topics might be part of an obedience assessment, because issues such as those are indeed important. But I believe the essence of obedience boils down to one issue, and Jesus would likely put it simply: Do you love one another?

If you want to get at the heart of obedience to Christ, that question must be the starting point. Before Jesus made His declaration linking love for Him and obeying His commands, He said, "A new command I give you: Love one another. As I have loved you, so you must love one another. By this everyone will know that you are my disciples, if you love one another" (John 13:34–35). Then a bit later in the same conversation, He reiterated the point. "My command is this: Love each other as I have loved you" (John 15:12).

Because this is such a critical aspect of obedience, let's look at specific ways to put love into action.

> To love people means forgiving them. Not just the people who are easy to forgive, but the most difficult people as well. The guy who stole your innocence? Yes. The person who vowed to spend forever with you and then abandoned you for someone younger? Yes. The boss who destroyed your career behind your back? Yes.

> To love people means seeking reconciliation with them. The family member who emotionally abandoned you in your moment of greatest need? Yes. The outspoken neighbor who publicly humiliated you? Yes. Your spouse whom you have separated from and are now planning to divorce? Yes. Let me be clear there are certainly scenarios when seeking reconciliation is unsafe. For instance, in relationships where abuse of any form has taken place, there could be great danger in seeking reconciliation. Beyond these unfortunate circumstances, as Christians, seeking reconciliation is the expectation.

> To love people means praying for those you consider enemies. Islamic terrorists? Yes. Political opponents? Yes. The estranged family member? Yes.

You want to live a life of obedience? You want to express your love for God? Love people. When it's easy and when it is not. When it's convenient and when it is not. When it is comfortable and when it is not. When it doesn't cost you anything and when it costs you everything.

Jesus's highest and greatest act of obedience had everything to do with loving people. The night Jesus would be arrested, after He had shared His final meal with His disciples, He traveled to the Garden of Gethsemane. To pray. To plead. To make one last appeal to His Father in hopes of determining another way to provide redemption that would not involve the cross. As He prayed, He was not play-acting. The Bible says He was sweating drops of blood. A medical doctor would tell you that sweating drops of blood is indicative of a condition called *hematidrosis*. This is a rare, but very real, medical condition in which one's sweat will contain blood. The sweat glands are surrounded by tiny blood vessels. These vessels can constrict and then dilate to the point of rupture, causing blood to enter the sweat glands. Its cause—*extreme* anguish.

In the garden, Jesus was not being dramatic; He was desperate. From the time He was laid in a wooden manger, He knew His path would lead to a wooden cross. He knew His life was going to inter-sect with a cruel death. But perhaps there was another way. Perhaps there was an alternative solution. Perhaps He could narrowly escape the cross and all it entailed. But not so. After realizing the inevitably of the cross, He spoke these words, "Father, … not my will, but yours be done" (Luke 22:42). Those are words of submission; those are words of obedience. Jesus's death on the cross had everything to do with obedience.

The cross was motivated by love for His Father and was an expression of His love for others. Obedience is not glamorous; it is often quite mundane. Obedience is simple, but rarely easy. Obedience is not the absence of love, but an expression of love. A love for God and for others.

9

BLATANT DEFIANCE

Jesus often drew lines in the sand.

You know the imagery of two people getting ready to fight on a playground, where one person draws a line not to be crossed. Battle lines are drawn, and sides have to be chosen. With a line in the sand, you are either left standing side by side with someone or standing face-to-face in opposition.

When you find Jesus drawing lines in the sand, the same people were always standing on the other side of the line in opposition—the religious crowd.

The question is why. If you didn't know any better, you would expect Jesus would be standing in opposition to the sinners, and by sinners we would probably mean people who struggle with so-called "big" sins. Yet that is the not the case. When Jesus found Himself in the midst of a dispute of some kind, His opposition was always the religious leaders of the day, people quick to judge and shame and condemn.

Why were the people you would expect to be aligned with Jesus often opposed by Him—and opposed to Him? Each encounter had specific reasons that caused Jesus to oppose the religious crowd, or vice versa, but two foundational issues seemed to keep showing up.

TRUE VALUES

First, Jesus valued people more than policies, while the religious crowd had it the other way around. As we read in Matthew 12,

> At that time Jesus went through the grainfields on the Sabbath. His disciples were hungry and began to pick some heads of grain and eat them. When the Pharisees saw this, they said to him, "Look! Your disciples are doing what is unlawful on the Sabbath." (vv. 1–2)

It should be said of the Pharisees that they were not complete villains. They helped to establish and enforce the spiritual laws of the land. Well educated and usually successful, they were some of the most respected people in all of society. If there was anyone you would have expected to be near and dear to God in the first-century Jewish world, it was the Pharisees.

In this passage there is mention of the Sabbath. In the Old Testament law, God gave instructions for the day called Sabbath, which was intended to be a day of rest and restoration. Naturally, there comes the question, "What qualifies as work and what qualifies as rest?" God provided specific instructions, none of which were intended to be oppressive. But over the years, the Jewish leaders added laws upon laws to ensure no one came close to breaking the rules. As a result, people had to work harder on the Sabbath than on any other day, just to stay in compliance. A day intended to be a blessing had turned in to a burden. Literally hundreds of Sabbath regulations were enacted, including these:

- No filtering undrinkable water to make it drinkable.
- No picking small bones from fish.
- No baking, cooking, or frying of food.
- No throwing objects in the air from one hand to the other, because that would constitute work.

So when the Pharisees saw the disciples violating one of their policies, they blew the whistle—thinking they also caught Jesus in a difficult spot. But Jesus took the opportunity to challenge them.

He answered, "Haven't you read what David did when he and his companions were hungry? He entered the house of God, and he and his companions ate the consecrated bread—which was not lawful for them to do, but only for the priests. Or haven't you read in the Law that the priests on Sabbath duty in the temple desecrate the Sabbath and yet are innocent? I tell you that something greater than the temple is here. If you had known what these words mean, 'I desire mercy, not sacrifice,' you would not have condemned the innocent. For the Son of Man is Lord of the Sabbath." (vv. 3–8)

In this response, Jesus made it quite clear that He had a different value system—in His view, people trumped policies. This seems to be a theme Jesus was intent on reinforcing. When He encountered a man with a shriveled hand, the Pharisees asked if it was lawful to heal on the Sabbath, seeking to catch Him in a trap (v. 10).

Jesus had a potential trap of His own. He asked those accusers what they would do if one of their sheep fell into a pit on the Sabbath—leave it to die or rescue it? Apparently, no one spoke up. So with that, Jesus healed the man's deformed hand (vv. 11–13).

Can you imagine sitting in the front row watching this scene play out? I don't know why or for how long this man's hand had been shriveled, but undoubtedly his disability had become part of his identity. It likely affected his ability to earn a living; it may have hindered his relationships and probably lowered his social status. And so his life was a story of disappointment, shame, and rejection … until he met Jesus. My imagination fills in some blanks, and I think the bystanders would have immediately erupted in applause. The healed man might have thrust both healthy hands toward the heavens, with Jesus smiling at the celebration. All the while, the religious leaders stood back, scowling, their hands clenched into angry fists. This can't be too far from the truth, for we read, "The Pharisees went out and plotted how they might kill Jesus" (v. 14).

TRUE TRANSFORMATION

Another pattern led to even more opposition between Jesus and the religious leaders: He valued *internal transformation* and they valued *external righteousness*.

There are many episodes in the Gospels where this dynamic emerged, but one of the clearest examples is found in Matthew 15. Pharisees tracked down Jesus in Jerusalem and asked why His disciples didn't follow religious tradition and wash their hands before eating.

> Jesus replied, "And why do you break the command of God for the sake of your tradition? For God said, 'Honor your father and mother' and 'Anyone who curses their father or mother is to be put to death.' But you say that if anyone declares that what might have been used to help their father or mother is 'devoted to God,' they are not to 'honor their father or mother' with it. Thus you nullify the word of God for the sake of your tradition. You hypocrites! Isaiah was right when he prophesied about you:

> "'These people honor me with their lips,
> but their hearts are far from me.
> They worship me in vain;
> their teachings are merely human rules.'"

> Jesus called the crowd to him and said, "Listen and understand. What goes into someone's mouth does not defile them, but what comes out of their mouth, that is what defiles them." (vv. 3–11)

If you wonder what, exactly, Jesus meant, you are in good company. His disciples didn't understand what He meant either, so a while later He explained.

> Don't you see that whatever enters the mouth goes
> into the stomach and then out of the body? But
> the things that come out of a person's mouth come
> from the heart, and these defile them. For out of the
> heart come evil thoughts—murder, adultery, sexual
> immorality, theft, false testimony, slander. These
> are what defile a person; but eating with unwashed
> hands does not defile them. (vv. 17–20)

Obviously, behavior matters, but only as it matches up with what is really going on inside. In another passage, Jesus tells the religious leaders that they are similar to whitewashed tombs—clean and beautiful on the outside but full of death and decay on the inside (see Matt. 23:27).

From the beginning of Jesus's ministry, He made it quite clear that what really mattered to Him was internal transformation. Early on, He delivered His famous Sermon on the Mount, which, multiple times, included the phrase, "You have heard it said …, but I tell you …." This was followed by an Old Testament command primarily focusing on external conduct, and He expanded it to include internal beliefs. Jesus took a law that seemed to be all about external righteousness and raised the standard to require internal transformation. He knew when a person's internal world is healthy and holy, the external will be also—but the opposite is not necessarily true. One can be completely morally compliant on the outside and all the while full of hatred, animosity, and decay on the inside.

When you focus on the external but the not the internal, you can get rid of the computer but still be immersed in pornographic fascination in the privacy of your heart and mind.

When you focus on the external but the not the internal, you can write a note of forgiveness and drop it in the mail but still nurture bitterness.

When you focus on the external but not the internal, you can offer congratulations with your lips but be full of jealousy and greed in your heart.

When you start thinking through the practical implications, it is not difficult to see why Jesus is primarily concerned about internal purity. For human beings, the emphasis is often on trying to clean up external behaviors, and here is why—it is much easier and less painful. It doesn't take much time and energy to whitewash the outside of a tomb, but to excavate the decay and death from the inside is not so easy.

UNCOMFORTABLE QUESTIONS

This whole discussion leads to an important question for you and me: Are we the "religious crowd" of our day?

The comfortable answer is no. The honest answer is yes.

In our culture, we are the type of people who would tend to be associated with God. People who show up to a local congregation. People who read the Scriptures. People who know what to say and when to say it. People who wear Christian T-shirts and have the bumper stickers on their cars. We are the religious crowd.

It is far easier to stay focused on the religious crowd of the first century and articulate the ways it missed out on who Jesus was. It isn't as comfortable when we turn the focus on ourselves. But doing so is necessary. You have likely heard the statement "If you don't learn from history, you are bound to repeat it." Wouldn't it be a great tragedy if decades from now people looked at this current generation and reflected how it was associated with God, but it never knew God? And by it, I do mean we. This idea may feel a bit abstract, as if we are dealing in shades of gray, but if Jesus showed up walking the streets again, the issue would quickly become black and white. Once again, He would begin to draw lines in the sand, and once again some people would be standing next to Him and others would be standing face-to-face with Him in opposition.

So who would be standing on the other side of the line? Surely, some would be people who are considered to be—or claim to be— the most religious. But there would be others. People who seem as though they have it all together on the outside. People who seem as though they have the Christian life figured out. People who sit next to you at church. People who read books like this one. People who write books like this one. People like you and me. I don't want to create a sense of paranoia or cause you to be hypercritical about your own life or the lives of others, but there is wisdom in honestly studying Jesus's life and then doing some self-evaluation.

Here is what we ultimately learn from studying the relationship dynamics between Jesus and the first-century religious crowd: it is possible to be closely associated with God without understanding the heart of God. The same thing happens today. Lots of believers attend church, join spiritual groups, read the Scriptures, and listen to acceptable radio programs. If we aren't careful and honest with ourselves, we could become like the religious crowd of Jesus's day. We might be so focused on doing and saying the right things that we overlook the importance of *being* the right people. The message of Jesus is that transformation happens from the inside out. Godly behavior will happen only when we pursue holiness and purity within our souls. We must seek to know the heart of God and let His truth and grace change our own hearts.

If we are going to know the heart of God, we can dwell on the two principles that caused such opposition for Jesus:

God cares about people more than policies.

God cares about internal transformation more than external righteousness.

How about you? Do you define spiritual maturity in your life and the lives of others based on things done or not done? Do you envision internal transformation as a journey completed or as a journey just begun? Which do you value more—the applause of people, prompted by outward behavior, or the applause of heaven, prompted by surrendering fully to God's transforming work?

Here is a simpler way to ask those same questions: When Jesus draws a line in the sand, where are you standing? Next to Him or in opposition to Him?

10

RECKLESS GRACE

People often ran to Jesus ... literally and figuratively.

When Jesus walked along the shores of Galilee and invited two fishermen named James and John to come with Him, they immediately left their nets behind and followed Him. In fact, they left everything behind—their livelihood and security—to follow Jesus. People were drawn to Jesus for many reasons, but the number one reason was grace.

RUNNING TOWARD GRACE

As you read about Jesus's life and ministry in the New Testament accounts, you will rarely come across the word *grace*, and yet grace is clearly on display nearly every time He interacted with people. As John wrote, "For the law was given through Moses; grace and truth came through Jesus Christ" (John 1:17).

I cannot help but think about a leper Jesus encountered. "When Jesus came down from the mountainside, large crowds followed him. A man with leprosy came and knelt before him and said, 'Lord, if you are willing, you can make me clean'" (Matt. 8:1–2).

Though we know very little about the man described, what we do know is all we really need to know. He had leprosy. Likely, those words do not make an appropriately heavy impression on our hearts and minds. We all experience medical challenges at some point in time, so it would be easy to think, *Oh, he had his challenges, but I have had my own*. I had the chicken pox, I've had nasty flu bugs, and on a more serious note, I suffer from asthma. We could each tell our own story of medical ailments and difficulties. And probably, every story we would have to tell would pale in comparison to the reality that was leprosy in the first century. Leprosy was not just an ailment or a medical challenge; it was a death sentence.

Leprosy is often misunderstood. It is perceived as being a bad rash or a really irritating skin condition, but ultimately leprosy is the inability to experience pain. To some, a painless existence sounds appealing, but that is only because we often miss out on the role that pain plays in our lives. Pain is a gift from God. Maybe pain is a gift you would rather do without, like the nose hair trimmer or gym membership or fruitcake you receive every Christmas, but it is a gift nonetheless. Pain serves as a protective mechanism for our bodies. When you touch a hot burner on the stove, pain alerts you to move your hand quickly. When you sprain your ankle, pain alerts you to change your gait to ensure no further damage is done. When you land in a belly flop from the high dive, pain alerts you to stay on the lounge chair where you belong. Pain protects. A leper feels no pain. So very quickly the body of a leper becomes covered with scrapes, scabs, and bruises, which develop into festering, infected wounds. Physical deterioration is inevitable and death is sure to follow.

Leprosy was a death sentence physically and also socially. Lepers were considered unclean, and they were required to live together in colonies far removed from the rest of society. In biblical times, lepers were required to wear a bell to warn others not to get close. Leprosy was a physical, emotional, and social affliction.

It was unusual, therefore, when the leper approached Jesus. It's likely that the assembled crowd let out a collective gasp. The leper knew he was breaking many social protocols, but something about Jesus made him feel welcome. Indeed he was, for Jesus said, "Be clean!" (v. 3). Immediately, the leper was cured. The Lord healed the man physically but did so much more in the process. Jesus could have simply spoken the words, and the healing would have still taken place. Yet we are told that He reached out and touched the man.

Being a leper, this man had likely not been touched by another human being in years, perhaps decades. Not a high five, not a pat on the back, not a hug. He was considered to be untouchable by everyone, everywhere … except Jesus. The crowd must have been shocked and stunned, but touching the untouchable wasn't an isolated incident for Jesus—it was a pattern; it was a lifestyle.

In the Gospels, we are given just a sneak peek into the life of Jesus, yet even so we find person after person who either touched Him or was touched by Him. The common motivation was grace, whether to give or to receive.

Think about the woman who had been bleeding for twelve years (see Mark 5:25–34). We are not told her name, perhaps intentionally. Her name was no longer her primary identity; her condition had become her identity. She was the bleeding woman. Whether she had been rich or poor, we do not know. But in either case, she had likely exhausted all her resources in a desperate search for a treatment, medicine, or therapy to cure her condition. Nothing had worked. Nothing had changed. Her blood caused her to be considered spiritually and socially unclean. And because she was unclean, undoubtedly she had been trapped in relational isolation for years. Perhaps at one point she had been married, but her husband would have abandoned her long ago. She would not have coworkers, because who would hire such a woman? It could be she had some siblings, but even they would have eventually backed away from her because of the cultural norms and expectations. Her heart was weary, her body was weak, and she was alone. She was destitute and desperate. She'd have to be to take the risk she took. As an unclean woman, she knew to keep her distance from other people. If she made contact, they, too, would become unclean. So she knew better.

I don't know what she had heard about Jesus, but something about who He was or what He had done convinced her to believe that her last shot, her only shot, was to get to Jesus. He was passing through the area, and with everything at stake, she pushed through the crowd, hoping to touch Jesus. And she did. She grabbed the edge of His cloak.

By law, her touch would have made Him unclean. By grace, just the opposite happened. Immediately, she was healed. Knowing that her highest and greatest dream had come true, she was likely hoping to slip back out of the crowd and resume a normal life. But Jesus didn't allow that to happen. He stopped and asked who had touched Him. Fear must have overwhelmed the woman's heart and mind. She had been caught.

As she trembled, Jesus looked through the crowd, trying to identify the culprit. He set His eyes on her, and He knew. He didn't rebuke; He rewarded her. He restored not only her health but also her dignity. We don't know what she had heard about Jesus, but after this pivotal moment, I have no doubt what others heard from her about Jesus: where there is Jesus, there is grace. As the word spread, it is no wonder so many people had the I-must-get-to-Jesus-whatever-it-takes mind-set. Lepers. Religious leaders. Children. Prostitutes. All running toward Jesus.

People should respond to Jesus's followers the way people responded to Him. That principle has many implications, but one is that the so-called untouchable people of your city and mine should come running to us because they know Jesus's followers will show them grace and love. Would people of your town or city be inclined to eagerly approach you? The better question—the more pressing question—is, *do* they eagerly approach you? Do the sick, the scorned, the social outcasts come running to you, knowing you will offer a warm embrace and a touch of healing?

If the answer is no, some alterations need to be made as followers of Jesus. Start with these two steps.

Expand Your Circle of Influence

Many of us develop social and relational circles that include people who look like us, talk like us, live like us, and believe like us. This most often happens subconsciously, not consciously. So to expand your circle will require you to make intentional decisions. Perhaps you could serve at a local soup kitchen, volunteer for a neighborhood cleanup project, participate in an English as a second language program, or work at a refugee center. The opportunities are endless, but these are choices we must make.

Will expanding your circle of influence be uncomfortable? Probably. Will expanding your circle of influence be convenient? Probably not. Have we been called to do so as Jesus followers? Absolutely. So find intentional ways as an individual, family, or community group to expand your circle of influence to include supposedly untouchable people.

So who is it in your community? Who is being ostracized or marginalized? Who is overlooked and undervalued? Illegal immigrants? The LGBT community? Inmates? Convicted felons? Heroin addicts? Registered sex offenders?

Who is it? Until you are willing to take the necessary time to answer the question, you will never expand your circle of influence. If you are brave enough to answer the question, then you can develop intentional plans to expand your circle of influence to include such people.

A couple of women I know founded a ministry called Woven 139. The ministry exists to restore dignity and meet the practical needs of transvestite prostitutes in our community. Transvestite prostitution is a multilayered, complex reality that I do not pretend to fully understand. Though the issue is complex, the mission of this ministry is simple—extend reckless grace. So these women have identified an area of our city where transvestite prostitutes linger, and the volunteers deliver healthy, hot meals and warm clothing. When everyone else simply looks the other way, these women are going out of their way to serve and love.

I am not suggesting that expanding your circle of influence means you need to drive around your town, community, or city looking for prostitutes, but it might. How far are you willing to go? How uncomfortable are you willing to get? What kind of risks are you willing to take? How reckless are you willing to be? Grace is worth it.

Look in the Mirror

You and I will never become an oasis of grace for others until we have a profound, life-changing encounter with God's grace. There are so many examples of Jesus's scandalous grace: the woman at the well who had already had five husbands and was living with her sixth … the woman caught in the act of adultery … the "sinful" woman who anointed His feet … the hated tax collector Zacchaeus, who became a dinner companion.

These stories have echoes in our own stories. We are all recipients of the most audacious brand of grace we could ever imagine. If we want to have a conversation about people who are untouchable because of their sin, we don't need to look to another area of town, or another zip code, or another time and place. We simply need to look in the mirror. We are people who not only struggled with sin, but also were dead in our sin before Jesus lavished us with His grace.

If you are a follower of Jesus, your grace story is summed up well by the apostle Paul.

> As for you, you were dead in your transgressions and sins, in which you used to live when you followed the ways of this world and of the ruler of the kingdom of the air, the spirit who is now at work in those who are disobedient. All of us also lived among them at one time, gratifying the cravings

of our flesh and following its desires and thoughts. Like the rest, we were by nature deserving of wrath. But because of his great love for us, God, who is rich in mercy, made us alive with Christ even when we were dead in transgressions—it is by grace you have been saved. And God raised us up with Christ and seated us with him in the heavenly realms in Christ Jesus, in order that in the coming ages he might show the incomparable riches of his grace, expressed in his kindness to us in Christ Jesus. For it is by grace you have been saved, through faith—and this is not from yourselves, it is the gift of God—not by works, so that no one can boast. (Eph. 2:1–9)

It is all too easy to learn about *how* you were saved and never understand *why* you were saved. The *how* is simple—God's grace. It is God's grace that sets us free from the penalty of sin, God's grace that washes away the shame that comes along with sin, and God's grace that redeems what was once broken and tattered because of our sin. But there is a need to understand the *why* of being saved. The very next verse in the Ephesians 2 passage says this, "For we are God's handiwork, created in Christ Jesus to do good works, which God prepared in advance for us to do."

The word *handiwork*, sometimes rendered *workmanship*, is translated from the Greek word that means "masterpiece." As someone who follows Jesus and has been saved by Jesus, you are a masterpiece. Every master designer has a masterpiece. You are God's masterpiece, and so am I. Like any masterpiece, we are made with a purpose. This is our purpose: we are saved by grace to share grace. The good works spoken about are essentially opportunities to dispense grace. We are grace dispensers—at least we are intended to be. When you think about the people who interact with you, are they more likely to experience guilt or grace? Grace, I hope.

When you are a follower of Jesus who sees the world the way He does, no one is untouchable, no one is unlovable. In fact, though Jesus didn't show favoritism and wouldn't want us to either, if there were people He most often rubbed shoulders with, it was people whom society deemed untouchable.

When I think about Jesus, I love the idea of Him literally rubbing shoulders with people, meaning He was among them, walked with them, and dined with them, so closely they would have brushed shoulders with one another. He was not content to stand at a distance; He drew near, close enough to touch people.

When Jesus established His church, He envisioned that His followers would live in such a way that hurting and broken people would come running to find a safe refuge. When people felt defeated and empty, they would find a group of believers to offer solace. When people reached the end of their ropes, they would come eagerly to a place of second chances and fresh starts.

THE INGREDIENT YOU CANNOT DO WITHOUT

I am not much of a cook. What I really mean is that unless it can be put on a grill or poured into a bowl with milk, I don't know how to cook. However, I have a general understanding of how cooking works. You choose a recipe and follow the instructions. Cooking sounds so easy when I articulate it that way. A good recipe takes out all the guesswork. You are told exactly what to use, how much of it to use, and when to use it.

A recipe becomes difficult when you don't have all the necessary items. With some recipes, you can probably switch out one ingredient for another, or a little less of this for a little more of that. However, in some cases, if you are missing even one ingredient, you need a new recipe altogether. For instance, if you are making sugar cookies without sugar, you better just find a new recipe. Sometimes there is one ingredient you simply cannot do without.

The same principle applies to grace and Christianity. You can't take grace out of the Christian faith recipe and replace it with something else. That is one essential ingredient. You take out grace, and then you need to call the church something other than the church, because where there is no grace, there is no church.

Grace is reckless, but more so, grace is required.

RADICAL HUMILITY

In an Ypsilanti, Michigan, psychiatric hospital, Dr. Milton Rokeach had three patients named Leon, Joseph, and Clyde. Their cases were unusual—they all suffered from a psychotic, delusional disorder called a Messiah Complex. Each one maintained that he was the reincarnation of Jesus Christ.

Rokeach spent two years working with the men, but change came hard. It was as if they couldn't bear to live if they discovered they weren't who they thought they were. With little to lose, Rokeach decided to try an experiment, placing the three men together in one small group. For two years, the three delusional messiahs were assigned adjacent beds, ate meals together, participated in the same tasks, and met daily for group therapy. Rokeach wanted to see if spending so much time with one another might provide a jarring reality check for the would-be messiahs. It was a kind of messianic twelve-step recovery program.

The experiment led to interesting conversations. During a particular group therapy session, one of the men declared, "I'm the Messiah, the Son of God. I am on a mission. I was sent here to save the earth."

Rokeach asked, "How do you know?"

"God told me," the man replied.

One of the other patients immediately chimed in, "I never told you any such thing!"

You might not know it, but the Messiah Complex is pretty common. Most people won't be officially diagnosed with the disorder, but they still have an inflated sense of their own importance and their place in the world, causing them to shape and arrange their entire lives around themselves.

I suppose this is as good a time as any to confess that I, too, have a Messiah Complex—not the psychiatric kind like Dr. Rokeach's patients have, but the condition is worth exploring. In fact, just about everyone struggles with a Messiah Complex to some degree.

Early scientists believed that the solar system revolved around the earth; now, of course, we know that the planets in our solar system revolve around the sun. Operating under a similar delusion, in our weak moments, we act as if the universe revolves around us. As people, we have the unique ability to make ourselves the center of everything. We expect special treatment, we act as if we are always right, and we have a me-first attitude, to name a few symptoms. As real as the Messiah Complex is, I believe the root cause is a deeper issue. The real issue is pride.

THE LASTING EFFECTS OF PRIDE

If we engaged in an exercise to list prevalent sins, almost all of us would include pride. In doing so, we would be accurate—sort of. Pride is indeed a sin, but it is also the root of every other sin. If you could revisit the Garden of Eden, you would find that it was pride that paved the way for sin. God had placed Adam and Eve in a literal paradise, teeming with magnificent sights, sounds, colors, tastes, and smells of every kind. God essentially said, "This is all for your enjoyment. Tend to creation. Be fruitful and multiply. Eat, drink, and be merry." In the midst of this vast array of opportunity, God gave just one restriction—a tree in the middle of the garden called the Tree of the Knowledge of Good and Evil. God instructed them, "Whatever you do, do not eat the fruit from that tree." We don't know how much time passed, but it wasn't long before Satan showed up in the form of a snake.

> Now the serpent was more crafty than any of the wild animals the LORD God had made. He said to the woman, "Did God really say, 'You must not eat from any tree in the garden'?" (Gen. 3:1)

The Bible says Satan is the father of lies, and not surprisingly, the first words we hear rolling off his forked tongue formed a twisted lie. With deception in his breath, he implied that God had said something He really hadn't. Eve was savvy enough to detect the deception, and she corrected the snake. "God did say, 'You must not eat fruit from the tree that is in the middle of the garden, and you must not touch it, or you will die'" (v. 3).

The snake took another run at trickery and insisted that she would not die and, in fact, would have her eyes opened and become like God. How differently eternity may have played out had Eve turned from Satan and his deceptive ways. But instead, her eyes lit up at Satan's promise, which was too good to be true. Eve was already experiencing life to the fullest. She experienced life free of any suffering, pain, disappointment, or regret. Her every need was met and every desire fulfilled.

With the lie lingering in her heart and mind, Eve listened to the voice shouting in the depths of her soul—"You can be like God"—and it was the voice of her own pride. She took a bite of the fruit, shared it with her husband, and instantaneously sin and death came crashing into life-giving creation. Ever since that moment, every man, woman, and child who has ever lived on this earth has wrestled with an unhealthy pride that says, "You don't have to live God's way—you can live your own way. You don't have to settle for worshipping God—you can be your own god." It is this mind-set that leads us to think the world resolves around us.

Nearly everyone has suffered from a pride problem. The exception is Jesus. We might say that the only person who did not struggle with a Messiah Complex was the Messiah. Jesus could have rightly said, "The world revolves around Me." He could have said, "I am God's gift to humanity." But He didn't say those things. He also could have rightfully and easily come in the form of a mighty warrior riding on the back of a stallion for the entire world to see. But He didn't. He could have come with an entourage and security detail. But He didn't. He could have taken up residence in the finest palace the world has ever seen. But He didn't. He came in the most vulnerable, humble manner we could imagine. He arrived in the back of a borrowed stall, far off the beaten path, beyond the spotlight of society, in the form of a helpless baby. This was the beginning of a lifetime marked by humility and servanthood.

When we understand that we are called to live out the same brand of humility, we recognize what a challenge it is for us. From the youngest age, we are taught to look out for number one. If we don't, who will? Some of the earliest words that appear in our vocabulary are *mine* and *more*. Those words and the sentiments behind them stay with us as we grow older. We learn, early on, not to settle for the bottom rung of the ladder. Do whatever it takes to climb to the top rung. The mantra of our society is "Be great. Be great!"

If we are transparent, we all admit that we aspire to greatness. I don't know anyone who says, "I want to live a life no one notices." In fact, there is nothing wrong with aspiring to greatness. Our struggle is often a false understanding of what it means to be great according to God's standards. In His kingdom, greatness is not about becoming more, but about becoming less. Greatness is not measured by things acquired, but by things given away. Greatness is not determined by status, but by service. As Jesus said, "The Son of Man did not come to be served, but to serve" (Mark 10:45).

When Jesus made this statement to His disciples, He was almost three years into His ministry. His earthly ministry was almost over, so it is interesting that He shares His purpose with them again. You would think by that point they understood who He was and what He was about. They had listened to the Sermon on the Mount in person, they had seen the miracles firsthand, and they had listened to Him pray with His Father in heaven. Yet only a few days before Jesus would enter Jerusalem for the final time, they needed a reminder about His purpose. Though Jesus had told them otherwise, the disciples expected Jesus to establish a physical, earthly kingdom. That is actually what the Jewish people had in mind as they were waiting for their Messiah to come. They believed the Messiah would come with power and might. They expected Him to come with a sword in one hand and a shield in the other. So the disciples thought it wouldn't be much longer before Jesus would flex His proverbial muscles and show everyone who He really was—the King.

Because of this belief, the disciples had been jockeying for position, to see which of them would be the greatest in the new kingdom. Two of them, James and John, were not shy about making a power play. They said to Jesus, "We want you to do for us whatever we ask.... Let one of us sit at your right and the other at your left in your glory'" (Mark 10:35, 37).

They said, in essence, "Jesus, in the next few days when You over take the city of Jerusalem with Your mighty power, when You are inaugurated as the new King and You are sitting on Your royal throne, we want to sit beside You." They asked Him for power, prestige, and prominence. In modern parlance, they asked for a corner office, a private jet, the chairmanships of influential committees, and complete access to the Oval Office.

Jesus simply responded, "You don't know what you are asking" (v. 38).

The Bible says that when the other ten disciples heard about this conversation they were angry with James and John. They might have been upset at the audacity of the request or possibility because they didn't get to Jesus first with a request of their own.

To help set the matter straight, Jesus told them,

> Whoever wants to become great among you must
> be your servant, and whoever wants to be first must

be slave of all. For even the Son of Man did not come to be served, but to serve, and to give his life as a ransom for many. (Mark 10:43–45)

That mind-set goes against the grain of our thinking today, just as it did for the disciples' thinking thousands of years ago. We are trained to believe and live in just the opposite fashion. Our culture teaches that greatness is all about being or having more, and yet Jesus says greatness is all about being less and having less.

This is a really easy idea to articulate, but an excruciatingly difficult life to live.

Even writing about this idea of becoming less feels wrong, backward, upside down. And indeed it is. Many people have talked about or written about the "upside down" way of Jesus. That phrase describes so well what it is like to live in His kingdom and follow in His footsteps. Everything we know to be right in our little kingdoms gets turned upside down in His kingdom. Jesus says seemingly absurd things, such as, "The last will be first, and the first will be last" (Matt. 20:16). So according to Jesus's philosophy, this whole idea of greatness equaling humility makes perfect sense.

KING OF THE HILL OR HUMBLE SERVANT?

When you were a child, did you ever play the game king of the hill? If you didn't, the game is just as it sounds. Players gather around a hill and then scratch, claw, bite, push, pull, and do whatever it takes to be the one standing on the hill when the game ends. But let's be honest—that is not a game that is restricted to the playground in elementary school. Isn't that what life looks like sometimes? As we grow up, the message ingrained in our minds is to chase hard after wealth, success, influence, and luxury. Do whatever it takes, and fight to be king of the hill.

The mentality of that game stands in stark contrast to what it means to follow Jesus. A life of radical humility is not an easy path to walk, but it is the path we've been called to. Jesus made Himself nothing and then turned to us as His followers and said, "Follow Me. Follow Me into obscurity. Follow Me into selflessness. Follow Me into an others-focused life. Follow Me into My kingdom; the way is paved with radical humility." However, if you follow the crowd instead of following Jesus on the narrow road, you will naturally find yourself straining for the next rung, dreaming about an impressive title, and scheming about how you can get the place of honor at the table. Following the crowd is comfortable, easy, and safe, but following the crowd leads in a specific direction—away from Jesus.

If this is a blueprint for how our lives are intended to look, how are we doing? To answer, consider the following questions:

- Is your life built upon finding more ways to be served? Or finding more ways to serve?
- Do you find yourself daydreaming about how to move higher on the proverbial ladder? Or how to move lower in practical ways?
- Are you striving to create additional layers of material comfort in your life? Or diligently working to reallocate possessions to those in urgent need?

Imagine that after you have died, a headstone is placed at your grave, and the etched epitaph reads, "Not to be served, but to serve." Now imagine if the people who knew you best and loved you most showed up to visit your grave and they read that inscription. How would they respond? Would they think, *That's not exactly accurate?* Or would they quietly nod their heads in agreement, recognizing how well those words captured your life story?

Each of us would love to have the words "Not to be served, but to serve" etched on our headstone. But even more important for followers of Jesus is to have those words etched on our hearts.

Serving instead of being served sounds so poetic, but it can end up being quite painful. Just consider Jesus. He came from heaven to earth to serve people, and the very people He came to serve placed Him not so gently on a cross. I am not suggesting that by living a life of selfless service that you are destined for persecution, but don't be surprised if it happens. The road paved with selfless service is the road less traveled; it is a road that leads against the flow of culture, a road marked by obscurity, and perhaps pain, but most importantly a road that leads to life.

Part III

INTIMACY

12
MONKEY SEE, MONKEY DO

"Be like Mike." In the mid-1990s, Gatorade issued the challenge, and I accepted. I fully intended to be like Michael Jordan.

When I was a little tyke, my stepfather built a basketball court behind our home, so in my mind, becoming like Mike was just a matter of time. However, for multiple reasons, imitating Mike was tough for me. Michael Jordan was at the peak of his career; he was a six-foot-six African American man who was a lean, mean scoring machine. As for me, I was a high school freshman standing five-foot-zilch and weighing seventy-five pounds.

I should have chosen someone else to imitate, perhaps a chess champion, but everyone wanted to be like Mike. So I spent hours and hours honing my dribbling abilities, practicing fadeaway shots, perfecting my layups, and pretending to dunk, all while wagging my tongue out of my mouth. I fully intended to have a long, illustrious basketball career and maybe lucrative endorsement deals, just like Mike. It was all going according to plan … until I got cut from the freshman team.

As I walked out of the gym that fateful night, I had no choice but to face the grim reality—I couldn't be like Mike. My inability to be like Mike was not for lack of identification. I knew his moves. I could explain his tendencies. I studied his training regime. My failure to be like Mike was, plain and simple, a matter of inability. Identification was simply not enough.

There's a similar issue when it comes to trying to imitate Jesus: identification simply is not enough. Identification certainly matters. As we have seen, if you improperly identify who Jesus is and what He is like, you are sure to fail in your imitation of Him. For instance, if you believe in and follow American Jesus (as we discussed in chapter 2), then your attempt at imitating Him will likely lead you down a road that could be called American Dream Parkway. Along the way, you will do everything you can to accumulate stuff, acquire status, and achieve all the trappings of success, because that is, allegedly, what Americans are supposed to do. All this comes under the guise of honoring American Jesus. You certainly will not be alone as you travel the road, but you will likely be disappointed by the destination.

If you believe in and follow Fundamentalist Jesus, then your attempt at imitating Him will likely be dominated by avoiding certain behaviors. You will get very good at keeping score, following rules, and maintaining a religious checklist.

The circumstances will vary, but misguided identification of Jesus will always result in misguided imitation of Him. In the last several chapters, we have looked at snapshots of Jesus in action for the sake of identification. But hundreds of chapters could be written and still just scratch the surface of identifying who Jesus is and what He is like.

My kids love to go to the zoo, and one of our favorite places is the chimpanzee exhibit. On a lucky day, one of the monkeys will come right up to the glass and stare at us face-to-face. When that happens, the crowd begins to make faces and hand gestures, hoping the monkey will imitate the behavior. It's a monkey's ability to imitate behavior that led to the common phrase "Monkey see, monkey do."

Identification of Jesus alone will only ever lead to a "monkey see, monkey do" approach to imitating Him. That might lead to some good deeds and perhaps even impressing people in the religious crowd, but you will fall short of the life Jesus intends for you. Yes, Jesus calls us into a life of imitation, but imitation that is relational, not mechanical, in nature.

That is why Jesus placed much more emphasis on being than doing. His initial invitation to His disciples to follow Him became a pattern for the next several years. They spent three years of life and ministry together. They traveled, ate, prayed, and taught together. Jesus knew what the disciples did not. They likely envisioned their time together on earth going on for many years, especially after Jesus began His earthly reign. When His physical life was nearing its end, Jesus was intentional to communicate His greatest desire for them.

The night He would be arrested, Jesus gathered them together to share a meal and then set off toward Gethsemane. It seems that on the journey from the room to the garden, they came upon a vineyard. Jesus seized a can't-miss opportunity to explain to His followers what He wanted most.

> I am the true vine, and my Father is the gardener.
> He cuts off every branch in me that bears no fruit,
> while every branch that does bear fruit he prunes
> so that it will be even more fruitful. You are

already clean because of the word I have spoken to you. Remain in me, as I also remain in you. No branch can bear fruit by itself; it must remain in the vine. Neither can you bear fruit unless you remain in me.

I am the vine; you are the branches. If you remain in me and I in you, you will bear much fruit; apart from me you can do nothing. If you do not remain in me, you are like a branch that is thrown away and withers; such branches are picked up, thrown into the fire and burned. If you remain in me and my words remain in you, ask whatever you wish, and it will be done for you. This is to my Father's glory, that you bear much fruit, showing yourselves to be my disciples. (John 15:1–8)

Repeatedly Jesus says, "Remain." You can hear "Remain with Me" as "Be with Me." Yes, there is a world to save. Yes, there is work to do. Yes, there are challenges that lie ahead. Yes, there will be difficulties. But first and always, remain. What Jesus wanted the most was not more *from* His followers but more *of* His followers. The distinction may seem slight, but it is actually seismic. Jesus was so repetitive and so emphatic in making this distinction because we so often gravitate to doing. We work, toil, and sweat, hoping to earn the right to be in relationship with Jesus. The intention is good, but the overwork is counterproductive. *Doing* doesn't lead to *being*.

Even if you set your heart and mind to mechanical imitation of Jesus, you would fail to do so. The strength, courage, wisdom, and love necessary to imitate Jesus flow from remaining in Him and staying connected to Him. Real compassion, simple obedience, reckless grace, and innumerable other qualities of what it is to be like Jesus will flow only from relationship. With that in mind, consider this question: Which do you spend more time and energy doing—learning to *know about Jesus* or learning to *know Jesus*?

MOVING BEYOND INFORMATION

Imagine the person you know more completely than anyone else in your life. What if you had that individual write out his or her life story, with all the interesting facts, compelling details, and captivating events? Then, when all the information was written down, you made copies, handed them out, and asked people to memorize the facts. If people memorized the information, do you think they would know the individual as completely as you do? I didn't think so. The same thing happens all the time with the Bible.

Consciously or not, many people approach the Bible in pursuit of information rather than in pursuit of relationship. Of course, I'm not saying there is no value in Bible study or learning new information. But if learning more *about* Jesus is the primary purpose of studying Scripture, then the effort is shortsighted. The issue with learning more biblical information depends on the motivation. If the motivation in Bible study is simply to become puffed up with knowledge, you might as well spend your time scrolling through Wikipedia.com. At least then you would be tough to beat in Trivial Pursuit or might one day qualify for Jeopardy. However, if your purpose in studying the Bible, especially Jesus's life, is for the purpose of deepening your relationship with Him, then study as much as you possibly can.

Perhaps this discussion about motivation seems a bit like splitting hairs, but it is not. The best intentions at times lead people away from God instead of nearer to Him. Exhibit A: the apostle Paul, formerly known as Saul. When he still went by Saul, he was an incredibly religious man. His résumé would have made grown men salivate. He was born into the right family that was part of the right tribe. Educated under the best religious teachers, he mastered the difference between right and wrong and lived accordingly. He likely figured if he ever encountered God walking down the road, God would break into loud and raucous applause.

Ironically, one day while Saul was traveling down a Damascus road, he did have an encounter with God—namely, Jesus (see Acts 9:1–9). The encounter was not physical, but spiritual. No applause could be heard. Instead, Jesus verbally called out Saul for working against the desires of God. Saul was essentially working as a religious terrorist. He had made a habit of persecuting, mistreating, and even killing people who were following the Way.

Jesus blinded Saul, who might have been on a mission to kill more. Then the words came: "Saul, why do you persecute Me?" He didn't say, "Why are you persecuting people who follow Me?" This was personal. As the story played out, Saul professed Jesus as Lord and Savior. Saul becomes Paul—a new name, a new identify, a new life mission.

So what had gone wrong? How had a man so intent on carrying out God's will ended up so far outside of it? Saul had learned all the information about God, but he had not been in relationship with God. He knew a lot about faith, but he didn't know the Source of faith. He contained significant head knowledge, but little soul connection.

Seeking information about God as opposed to seeking to deepen relationship with God makes all the difference in how our faith is lived out. Information about Jesus matters. Identification of Jesus matters. But not in the absence of relationship with Jesus.

13
WITH

Every relationship requires definition. Acquaintance. Coworker. Imaginary friend. Neighbor. Secret admirer. Fiancé. Spouse. Child. Parent. Second cousin, twice removed. Without definition, relationships can become confused or even derailed because of unmet expectations. Where there are unmet expectations *in* the relationship, there is certain to be lack of fulfillment *from* the relationship.

How a relationship is defined determines how you interact with, communicate with, invest in, and respond to the other person. For instance, I have a very different relationship with my mail carrier than I do with my sister. You probably do as well, unless your mail carrier happens to be your sister. I also have a different relationship with my sister than I do with my children. And of course I have a different relationship with my children than I do with my wife. Because expectations are known in these relationships, I am better able to understand my role and response.

DEFINING THE RELATIONSHIP

So how would you define your relationship *with* Jesus? How do you view your role in the relationship respective to His? Perhaps defining your relationship with Jesus feels like a matter of overthinking and overanalyzing. Isn't the fact that you have a relationship with Jesus sufficient?

Many people claim to have a relationship with Jesus, and yet the role they envision Him playing in their lives is not a role He offers to play. The supposed roles for Jesus are many, but let me name a few. In relationship to your life or mine, Jesus is not …

An Add-on Feature

I have owned quite a few cars, some clunky and old, others nice and new. Now that I am a father of three, we lean toward the safe, conservative, and spacious. But I have experienced the other side. I try to avoid car dealerships because I find the "new-car smell" intoxicating. If you have ever shopped for a new car, you know you can easily become overwhelmed with all the possibilities of add-on features. Fog lights. Seat warmers. Navigation system. Moonroof. Sunroof. Alloy wheels. Leather seats. DVD players. The list goes on and on.

Each feature is something extra, designed to improve the experience, enrich the interior environment, and draw admiring looks from other drivers. The add-ons each come with a promise—to make your vehicle faster, safer, more comfortable, more impressive, more efficient, or more convenient. Each feature makes a specific and unique promise, but they all promise to make the car *better*.

Jesus often gets peddled similarly to an add-on feature for a car. With Him, your life will be better. Other promises get attached to Jesus too—wealth, health, success, prestige, comfort. I understand why Jesus gets talked about in this way; it makes Him sound so appealing, desirable, and necessary. So I recognize why Jesus gets packaged the way you might offer an accessory or add-on for a car. But there is just one problem. Jesus is not an add-on feature. He is not merely available to be added on, in hopes of experiencing a better life, whatever that may mean for you. Thinking about Him in such a way not only cheapens who He is, but also completely misses out on who He is.

A Drawer

Many people have a natural tendency to compartmentalize their lives. Think, for example, of your life as a dresser with multiple drawers. Each drawer represents the various parts of your life. Drawers are labeled "Career," "Finances," "Family," "Friendships," and "Hobbies." For most people, the drawers would be the same, with one or two interchanged. There is another drawer that many people include. "Religion." It represents a person's beliefs, activities, and commitments. For some people, the label "Religion" wouldn't seem quite right, so they would label it "Jesus." In that drawer, they would store their beliefs, expectations, and feelings about Jesus.

Having a drawer labeled "Jesus" sounds noble and admirable unless you ask Jesus what He thinks. What He would say might surprise you. I cannot speak for Jesus, but this is what I *think* He would say: "I refuse to be a drawer in your chest of drawers. I don't want to be one among many categories in your life-dresser."

As generous as it might seem to allow Jesus to be one of the drawers in our life, He is unwilling to occupy that limited role. Though the offer to include a Jesus drawer is made with the best of intentions, He is not impressed, certainly not flattered, and probably offended. He refuses to be reduced down to a compartment, even if it is the top drawer.

When you enter into relationship with Jesus, you don't add Him into your chest of drawers. You don't decide His place; He decides yours. You don't make room for Him; He makes room for you.

An Insurance Policy

Many people have a tremendous fear of the unknown. For some, this means worrying about what will happen next week, next month, or next year. For others, the fear pertains to what comes after this life. If you're one of them, you are certainly not alone. What exactly will the afterlife be like? When will my time come? Will I be ready? Because we rely so much on our five senses, we become uneasy, even fearful, about the inability to investigate what comes next. That is why many bestselling books describe what the afterlife will hold. Whether they feature a little boy who experienced heaven and came back to tell about it, or someone who claims to have tasted the torture of hell, people are fascinated with these stories.

Perhaps because there is so much unknown about the afterlife, some people treat Jesus as though He is an eternal insurance policy. They think, *I don't know much about heaven or hell. I am not even sure if hell is real or not, but if I just have a dose of Jesus in my life, then I will be covered just in case.* Though people probably do not think about Jesus this way on a conscious level, plenty of them keep Him around "just in case." He's not a life insurance policy but an afterlife insurance policy.

An Audience

Oftentimes during my journey of faith, I have heard people use the phrase "Audience of One." I have heard that language used in prayers, seen it printed on T-shirts, and listened to it used in well-intended sermons. Be reminded, the saying goes, you are performing for an audience of One. So the imagery is of you on the stage and Jesus sitting in a comfortable theater chair or perhaps up high in a luxury box. In either case, you are in the spotlight, trying to execute the right choreography and recite the appropriate lines. Of course, you're hoping to receive applause. If you do really well, perhaps you'll get a standing ovation.

Though Jesus is extremely interested in your life, He is not interested in having you perform for Him, even if you have the best of intentions. If you perceive your relationship with Jesus in such a way, you will almost certainly feel like a failure. That's because you will inevitably miss a step here and there or forget a line.

An Instructor

In the Gospels, Jesus is referred to multiple times as a rabbi, and appropriately so. Jesus taught—often. He taught crowds of people, small groups, and individuals. He continues to teach us thousands of years later through His Word. His teaching was thought provoking, faith challenging, heart tugging, and life changing. As His followers, we should regularly experience His teaching as guidance and inspiration for our daily lives.

The danger comes when people think of their relationship with Jesus primarily in teacher-student terms. So essentially their role is that of a student sitting at a desk, furiously writing notes, while Jesus is the wild-haired professor hurriedly lecturing through a lesson plan. Because this perspective of the relationship is based on learning, knowledge becomes the measurable element. The more the better. As mentioned previously, if our focus is on knowing *about Jesus*, we might not get to *know Jesus*. Though continual learning is a must in any relationship with Jesus, He is not just a teacher; He wants to be your loving Lord, faithful friend, and closest ally.

CREATING A HEALTHY RELATIONSHIP

We've seen that Jesus is not an add-on feature, a drawer, an insurance policy, an audience, or an instructor. Nor is He a dose of religion, a convenient helper, or a spiritual genie in a bottle. We know lots of roles that Jesus doesn't want to play in our lives. Which leads us to ask exactly what kind of relationship He desires to have with us.

So what is the right imagery that communicates the nature of the relationship we have been invited by Jesus to share with Him? A love affair. Yes, really. Intimacy with Jesus.

That imagery and implication may sound a bit extreme, but it is biblical. Throughout Scripture, God uses intimacy language to communicate His love for people. In the Old Testament, God used references to adultery to talk about His people turning to other, lesser gods. In the New Testament, He could have used any label in reference to His church. Acquaintance. Admirer. Religious associate. Instead, He chose the word *bride*. Not by accident, but by design. There is intimacy implied behind that label. You are the one He has chosen. You are the one He desires to know in the most intimate of ways. He is not content to stand at a distance and wave. He wants to draw near.

Jesus could have stayed in the comfortable, luxurious, safe confines of heaven and invited His followers into a long-distance relationship. But He did not. Jesus drew near in the most literal way imaginable, so near that He could be seen, smelled, and touched. When He came, He did not retreat from people. He pursued them. He invited people to know Him and to be known by Him.

Have you ever taken the time to observe a longtime married couple? Perhaps a couple that has been married for fifty, sixty, or even seventy years. If you have, almost certainly you have witnessed a husband and wife who regularly finish each other's sentences, use similar facial expressions, and exhibit similar idiosyncrasies and habits. Perhaps you have even observed that some couples begin to look alike. Why does this pattern develop? Intimacy leads to imitation. The couples have spent months, years, and decades experiencing intimacy with each another, not just sexually, but also emotionally and spiritually. They have grown intimate with each another in every aspect of the word; almost literally, two have become one.

That is the picture of the relationship we are invited to share with Christ. A life, in the most literal fashion, defined by intimacy.

Real imitation of Jesus will only and always flow from real intimacy with Jesus.

It is no wonder the church is called the bride of Christ, because though intimacy can certainly be experienced at some level outside of a marriage relationship, the fullness of intimacy is best experienced within the confines of a marriage.

Almost eleven years ago I first met my wife when I attended a worship concert at a church in Louisville, Kentucky. Afterward, I received an invitation to join a night of food and games at the house of a young woman named Alex. For the previous several months, I had been teaching an adult Bible study, and one of the women in that class told me about a girl named Alex she wanted me to meet. She had said, "She loves Jesus and you love Jesus—you will be perfect for each other." If only it were that easy, right?

The evening at the worship concert, I recognized the name Alex and wondered if *this* Alex was *that* Alex. I asked to be introduced to her. A few moments later, we shook hands and—cue the music here—a love story began. Ten months later we were married and committed to spend our lives together. As I reflect on our first decade of marriage, I recognize that intimacy is not defined by a moment or even a collection of moments, but intimacy is the very nature of our relationship.

Intimacy is physical, but is also and always so much more.

Intimacy is knowing and being known.

Intimacy is pursuing and being pursued.

Intimacy is discovering and being discovered, over and over again.

Intimacy is listening and being listened to.

The same is true in relationship with Jesus. Intimacy with Jesus is not achieved in a moment, and it isn't defined by a few select moments. Intimacy is the very nature of the relationship Jesus desires to share with us. Feelings may come and go, passion may rise and fall, but intimacy should define our relationship with Jesus at every level.

Here is where the intimacy with Jesus becomes so unique—we were known fully and completely by Him before we ever became aware of His existence. Psalm 139 says it is God who knit us together in our mother's wombs. From before the time we were conceived, Jesus has known us, but our knowing of Him did not begin until later. For some people, knowing Jesus begins early in life; for others, knowing Him does not begin until much later in life. In either case, our intimacy with Jesus is exceptional because He doesn't need to get to know us, but we need to get to know Him. Yet He was not content to sit back in the confines of heaven, hoping we would somehow find Him.

He came. He drew near. So He could be known. By you. By me. By us. Intimately.

14
SOMETHING

There was something about Jesus.

I would prefer to use more compelling language to describe Jesus's compelling nature, and yet I am always left with these simple words. There was something about Jesus.

During Jesus's ministry, people constantly surrounded Him, clamoring for Him. All kinds of people. Rich. Poor. Sick. Well. Overlooked. Undervalued. Successful. Destitute. Religious. Pagan.

Sometimes the crowds lingered for hours as Jesus taught; other times they stayed only momentarily as Jesus passed from one village to the next. But in either case, at some point the crowds dispersed, and—I cannot prove this, but I believe—one of the most common phrases uttered as people returned home would have been, "There is something about Jesus."

And there was.

There was something about Jesus that compelled a wealthy, wee little man named Zacchaeus to climb a tree in hopes of merely catching a glimpse.

There was something about Jesus that compelled James and John to leave their nets and boat behind to follow Him.

There was something about Jesus that compelled a bleeding woman to push through the crowds, hoping to touch His robe.

There was something about Jesus that caused a Samaritan woman to leave behind her water jug and go tell everyone in town about the new man she had met.

There was something about Jesus that compelled Matthew to abandon his tax-collecting booth.

There was something about Jesus that compelled a religious leader named Nicodemus to risk his position and reputation by paying Him a visit in the night.

There was something about Jesus that compelled a thief on a cross to cry out for mercy.

The *something* about Jesus always caused people to take a second look at Him and get one step closer to Him.

You could chalk up this *something* about Jesus to His gracious disposition, joy, mercy, love, kindness, compassion, and commitment to justice. He possessed these qualities and many others that drew people to Him like a magnet. He still does.

Since Jesus returned to heaven more than two thousand years ago, how could He still have these qualities? The effect Jesus had on people during His time on earth is the same effect Jesus's followers should have on people now. A friend of mine has often said, "If you are following Jesus, then people should respond to you the same way they responded to Him." I agree. People responded to Jesus in a variety of ways. Some mocked Him. Some dismissed Him. Some ignored Him. Some debated with Him. Some beat Him.

But many people—most people—He came into direct contact with could not resist the magnetism of His overwhelming love, grace, and compassion.

As you experience intimacy *with* Jesus and live in imitation *of* Jesus, people should be left thinking, or even saying out loud, "There is something about _____ [insert your name]." These people likely will struggle to specifically identify what the something is about you. They may chalk it up to your gracious disposition, joy, mercy, love, kindness, compassion, or commitment to justice. This response from others is not just a silver lining that comes from imitating Jesus or a peripheral result of doing so. Instead, this response from others is woven into the very purpose of living in imitation of Jesus.

Experiencing intimacy with Jesus and seeking to imitate Him not only have everything to do with you but also have everything to do with others. Yes, Jesus desperately desires the deepest and most meaningful relationship with you, but not just with you. He is calling all people to Himself—the rich, poor, overlooked, undervalued, successful, destitute, religious, and pagan.

Living in imitation of Jesus is not just about one moment in time, but one moment after another after another. As you live in imitation of Jesus, people will often respond by taking a second look at you and moving one more step toward you. Clearly, the goal is not for people to be mesmerized by you but to meet Jesus because of you.

John the Baptist had an uncanny ability to draw people to himself—in part because he was a wild-haired zealot, but mostly because he shared a compelling message of God. When people flocked to him, there was opportunity to grab the glory and fame, but he always pointed toward Jesus. One time, a crowd of religious leaders gathered around John the Baptist and let him know that Jesus and His disciples were gaining more disciples than he was. Apparently, these leaders were trying to stir up competition and a turf war, tempting John to flex his influential, prophetic muscles and regain the spotlight. It didn't work. John was pleased and relieved at the news that Jesus was gaining fame, saying, "He must become greater; I must become less" (John 3:30). Previously, people had come to him, wondering if he was the promised Messiah. Again, avoiding the opportunity to build his own reputation and fame, he said, "I am not the Messiah.... I am the voice of one calling in the wilderness, 'Make straight the way for the Lord'" (John 1:20, 23). Every time, John pointed the eyes of people to Jesus.

POINTING THE WAY

One of my best friends is named Paul, who happens to be a federal agent. Recently, his wife called him to ask about significant purchases that had showed up on their bank statement. Soon, they concluded that someone else made the purchases, especially once Paul realized his debit card had gone missing. He quickly realized he had left the card in one of the pneumatic delivery tubes at a local pharmacy. Likely, a person who followed after him had taken the card.

Paul set out on the investigative trail, and being a federal agent, he had ample means to do so. Security footage was watched, background checks performed, addresses searched; and within a matter of hours, Paul sat in front of the home of the man who had used his card for a wild shopping spree. If Paul were not a follower of Jesus, the story at this point might have taken a different direction. Paul admitted he was tempted to inflict significant and perhaps appropriate punishment on the thief, but that is when he sensed Jesus nudging him to demonstrate grace and forgiveness.

After Paul introduced himself, which included flashing his federal badge, the man realized he was at Paul's mercy. Though Paul certainly addressed the seriousness of breaking the law, he chose to extend grace. The merciful act caused the man to step forward and embrace Paul in a tearful hug. Paul responded appropriately and accordingly—he pointed the man's eyes toward Jesus. I don't know how the story will end, but I do know that the next Sunday, as I stepped to the platform to preach, I looked out to see the man sitting next to Paul in the pew.

Sam was a third-generation addict—a predisposition for substance abuse was in her DNA. While other children grow up discovering new toys, Sam grew up discovering new drugs. She was given alcohol and pot as early as eight years old. Drugs were only part of the trauma she experienced. Tragically, her biological father molested her at a young age. The emotional and physical pain of the event was difficult enough, but even more difficult was that no one believed her. From there, life continued to unravel at the seams.

When Sam was fourteen, her grandmother gave her hard-core drugs. The same year, she gave Sam to a twenty-six-year-old man. For four years, he sexually, physically, and emotionally abused her. He kept her locked in an abandoned trailer for months, with only cold running water. She was totally dependent on him and had very little interaction with anyone else. During this four-year nightmare, Sam's abuser became the father of her first child, Ranae.

After a series of events, Sam was ordered to rehabilitation; and that is when Chris, a female member of our church, met her for the first time. She was immediately drawn to Sam and had a deep love and concern for her. Though Sam was in rehab, Chris knew she would need so much more. Sam needed a family. Sam needed hope. Chris offered her both. After the stint in rehab, Chris and her husband, Randy, invited Sam to make their home her home, no strings attached. And she did. They quickly learned Sam had an infant daughter who had been taken from her and was living in foster care.

For several months, Chris worked with state agencies to secure a reunion between Sam and her daughter. Of course, the court mandated that if Sam were going to be awarded custody, she would need to prove she had a stable living situation. Now, she could do just that. Over the next several months and years, Chris and Randy loved Sam and her daughter completely and intentionally, a kind of love she had never experienced before. She had known lust, but she had never truly known love. This love caused Sam to take a second look at Chris and Randy and a step toward them. Not surprisingly, this couple redirected Sam's eyes—and her feet—toward Jesus. Today, Sam is not only clean and sober, happily married, and the mother of two children, but also a devoted follower of Jesus.

My "big" sister Jenni—who is five-feet tall and weighs ninety pounds, dripping wet—moved to Southeast Asia. Not just for fun or adventure, but because she felt led to play an active role in fighting the injustice of human trafficking. She may be small in stature, but she is a spiritual giant. Jenni is the director of a group home for girls rescued from sex slavery. Occasionally, she will share with me a story of what God is up to in her circle of influence. Recently, she sent me an email about a girl she called Hope.

> We got a call late one Friday night a few weeks back to pick up a girl at the police station. She had been found on the road outside the city and brought in to the care of local authorities. At the time, she was drugged and very afraid. I've never seen the look of "wild-eyed terror" like I saw in her eyes that night.
>
> We don't know much about Hope. We don't know her real name, her age, where she came from, or if she even has a family. When she arrived at [our home] that first night, and over the next several days, she demonstrated severe erratic behavior and had to be monitored at all times. She wouldn't speak, she ripped her clothes apart when she got upset, and destroyed everything she got her hands on. She didn't know how to use the toilet and had no concern for her personal cleanliness.

We knew we were not equipped to take her on long-term. When the staff took her for a medical checkup, she wouldn't cooperate and hospital staff said she needed to be admitted into a psych clinic. The plan was to keep her until we could find a long-term place for her, but we were concerned there would be no suitable place. As it turned out, we came up on a public holiday that made for a long weekend, so we had to wait—and we prayed. I didn't know what to pray except, "Jesus, help us help her." My coworker expressed that she could not rest at all during the holiday. She prayed and begged God, with tears, to show us what to do.

The only way to explain what happened next is that God heard our prayers and intervened. About a week into her stay with us, Hope's behavior completely changed. She became obedient and respectful toward the staff and others. She started talking and joining in activities with the other girls. She ate properly at mealtimes and cleaned up her dishes. She did her own laundry, bathed, and learned how to use the toilet.

The other girls embraced Hope and taught her how to live with us. Turns out, she is a smart girl who was lost inside of her desperate need for self-protection. Hope has begun sharing with our counselors about the severe, long-term trauma she has experienced. She has expressed fear that we will send her away. She says that as long as she gets food every day, she wants to live here forever.

Our staff assures her that she is safe, that we will not send her away. She begged to go to church with the girls this past Sunday and our staff said she was raising her hands and shouting, "Thank you, God, for bringing me here."

I cannot pretend to know the thoughts that are racing through Hope's heart and mind, but I also cannot help but wonder if, in her most private thoughts, she has pondered, *There is something about Jenni and her staff.*

There is something about Paul.

There is something about Chris and Randy.

There is something about Jenni and her coworkers.

Because there was and is something about Jesus.

The story can play out a million and one different ways, and the specifics don't really matter. What matters is that you live in intimacy with Jesus so that you will naturally live in imitation of Jesus. When you do, you will have the opportunity to point people's eyes and their feet toward Jesus.

INTIMACY + IMITATION = INVESTIGATION

When you are given the opportunity to introduce people to Jesus, some of them will be compelled to investigate Him. Perhaps you will know of their investigations, but many times you will not.

Investigations may be slow and steady, or quick and urgent. They may be short lived or long term. They may be private or public. They may begin clamoring for answers to hard questions and chasing after eternal truths, wondering how someone could really return from the dead.

Surely, some who investigate Jesus will turn away. Others will reject the unmistakable evidence of His resurrection and worthiness to provide salvation. Some will simply grow disillusioned along the way. Some may put their investigation on hold until a later time. But for others, the investigation of Jesus will result in experiencing intimacy with Jesus. And intimacy with Jesus always leads to imitation of Jesus.

This whole idea of multiplication is not merely a nice by-product or bonus for people of faith; it is the core mission of anyone who follows Jesus. We have been given the instruction by Jesus to multiply followers.

> Therefore go and make disciples of all nations,
> baptizing them in the name of the Father and
> of the Son and of the Holy Spirit, and teaching
> them to obey everything I have commanded you.
> (Matt. 28:19–20)

This statement from Jesus can be analyzed and explained in endless ways, but the core of this message is simple and unmistakable: go and multiply. Interestingly, this final command of Jesus is a mirror image of one of God's first commands to humanity. To Adam and Eve, He said, "Be fruitful and multiply."

Jesus's invitation to live in intimacy with Him and imitation of Him centers on this mission. So this whole journey of properly identifying Jesus is not about being right or wrong; it is about fulfilling the mission for your life. That is why we cannot settle for Counterfeit Jesus, but must relentlessly pursue Real Jesus of the Bible.

FINAL THOUGHTS

So now you will do with this book whatever you do with books when you are finished. Put it on the shelf to collect dust. Give it away. Sell it at a garage sale. Use it as a coaster. Regardless, now that you are finished, you will move on to the next book, the next article, or the next Bible study. You will move on. And you should.

Though your journey through the pages of this book is complete, I hope your journey of discovering truth will continue, with great intentionality and purpose. Never let the dust gather on your image of who Jesus is and what He is like, as well as what He has called you to do and be. My prayer is that you will forever be developing a new and fresh picture of Jesus—Real Jesus. Even more importantly I pray that you will forever be developing a new and fresh passion for Jesus and your relationship with Him.

Reflect and Discuss
A STUDY GUIDE FOR GROUP AND INDIVIDUAL USE

CHAPTER 1: LIKE JESUS

1. What did "becoming a Christian" mean to you earlier in your life? How has your understanding of what it means changed?

2. Consider the command of Jesus in the New Testament to men He was challenging to become His disciples: "Follow Me." With what questions might they have wrestled? For example, "Does He know who I am and what I've done?"

3. Jesus, Son of God, invites you today to follow Him. Be candid! What objections do you have to that invitation?

4. Are you ready to be "covered in the dust of the Rabbi"?

Prayer

Father, I know You never gave a command that was impossible for Your servants to obey. Therefore, help me understand and believe by faith that it is You who will provide the power to follow Your Son, day by day, in order to be transformed into His image. Thank You, Jesus, for calling me to be one of Your many disciples.

CHAPTER 2: BUILD-A-JESUS

1. As you read the author's list of possible "Jesus types," which one did you identify with the most?

2. Which type of Jesus did you like the most?

3. In Matthew 25, Jesus set a high premium on "knowing Him," which of course means having a relationship with Him. Is it possible to worship a false image of Jesus instead of the real Son of God?

4. Have you ever read through just one of the Gospels (Matthew, Mark, Luke, or John) and built a composite picture of the Jesus of the Bible? Consider reading just two chapters of any of the Gospels and jot down His attitudes, character, commands, and actions. Maybe then you could compare the biblical Jesus to the type of Jesus you may have unintentionally built for yourself.

Prayer

Dear Father, I sincerely want to know, worship, and serve Jesus of Nazareth, Jesus of the Scriptures, not the Jesus of my own making. Help me, Holy Spirit, through study, to become better and better acquainted with Jesus of the Bible and thereby worship and follow Him, the only Son of God. I long to be a real disciple of Real Jesus.

CHAPTER 3: COUNTERFEIT

1. If Jesus were to meet you today at a coffee shop, would you be excited, nervous, horrified, delighted, or worried? Elaborate.

2. Based on Jesus's identity in the Bible, if He decided to visit your city, where would He likely go? What people or groups of people might He spend time with?

3. As you consider meeting with Jesus, would you welcome a heart-to-heart talk with Him? Would you accept a hard conversation about your sin, or would you rather Jesus not evaluate your relationship with Him?

4. Would you diagnosis yourself with "spiritual paranoia"? If so, what is your prescription for getting rid of it?

Prayer

Lord God, I want to be real with You all the time. Forgive me when I play games with my relationship with You. Help me get a handle on my Savior's true identity as revealed in the Bible. Make me sensitive to the areas in which I am failing and falling short. I know I have everything to gain by knowing Real Jesus. Surely I have nothing to lose except my momentary, childish concept of Christ—who willingly died so I could be forgiven and rightly related to You for time and eternity.

CHAPTER 4: REBUILDING

1. In your relationship with Jesus, who is doing the imitating? Counterfeit Jesus or you?

2. Have you had an "honest admission" on your spiritual journey? Explain.

3. Recall the lines from the following children's song: "The wise man built his house upon the rock.... The foolish man built his house upon the sand." Is your "house" built on the rock or on the sand? Do you need to rebuild?

4. Start now with a clean slate. How will you begin?

Prayer

Dear Jesus, it is my desire to know who You really are. Please allow me to clear my heart and mind of all preconceived ideas of who You are. No one can replace You in my life. Guide me away from looking to others to fill needs only You can cover.

CHAPTER 5: HOLY ANGER

1. What would your "Build-A-Jesus" look like? What characteristics would He have?

2. Does anything make you mad enough to do something about it in the name of Jesus? Explain.

3. Do your emotions mirror the emotions of Jesus? Which ones are alike? Which ones are different?

4. Be honest. Have you found yourself judging others by their life choices? Have you ever thought, *I would never end up like that*? How can you more fully and graciously accept people right where they're at?

Prayer

Jesus, I come to You asking for You to light a holy fire in my heart for the oppressed and downtrodden. Lead me to those who desperately need to see

You, Jesus. I want to serve them with the compassion and love that could come only from You.

CHAPTER 6: REAL COMPASSION

1. Have you "seen Jesus"? In a homeless person? In a child? In an elderly person?

2. What does compassion look like to you? Describe a time when compassion was shown to you. How did your experience make you want to show compassion to others?

3. If you tried to list how many times you felt compassionate and how many times you acted on that compassion, would the list be equal?

4. Think of specific ways you can show compassion to someone. Don't limit yourself. Don't limit Jesus.

Prayer

Dear God, thank You for giving me many examples in Scripture of Your Son showing compassion to others. May I allow those examples to lead me to act swiftly and love unconditionally. Break my heart for what breaks Yours.

CHAPTER 7: MESSY LOVE

1. Read 1 Corinthians 13 and write down all the words Paul uses to describe what love is.

2. To love like Jesus often means accepting situations that aren't neat and tidy. Give examples of messy love.

3. Have you had any divine interruptions lately? If so, what were they and how did they turn out?

4. Imagine the scene described in Mark 2 of the paralytic man and his four friends. This story takes the word *friend* to a whole new level. Do you have a friend such as this? Are you a friend like this?

Prayer

God, thank You for turning something messy into something beautiful. You've known me since the beginning of time, and I pray I'll spend the rest of my life getting messy being the hands and feet of Christ. Your love is like none other. Help me have a 1 Corinthians 13 love. Thank You for sending Your Son, Jesus, to demonstrate what perfect love looks like by making the ultimate sacrifice. "He gave His life as a ransom for many."

CHAPTER 8: SIMPLE OBEDIENCE

1. Are you a compliant person? Would your family and friends say you are compliant?

2. While Jesus was fasting and praying in the desert for forty days, Satan tempted Him. We all face temptations regularly. What tempts you?

3. Each time Jesus was tempted by Satan, He responded with Scripture. Can you recall Scripture passages when you are tempted? A helpful tool is to write a scripture on a sticky note and put it in a place you will see it regularly, such as the bathroom mirror or refrigerator. Memorize it, and then once you have committed it to memory, write down a new one. Before you know it, you will have memorized quite a few verses. Which scriptures will you begin memorizing?

4. What is God's general will for your life? Are you obeying God daily or just when it's convenient for you?

Prayer

Jesus, I want to obey You in every part of my being. When I am tempted, give me strength to turn my back on Satan and run toward You. You have promised that You will never leave me or forsake me. Allow me to experience Your love and not generalize it into something it was never meant to be. I desire Your deep love that knows no shallow territories.

CHAPTER 9: BLATANT DEFIANCE

1. Describe a time in your childhood when you were blatantly defiant. Have you had a similar experience as an adult? How are they the same? How are they different?

2. Give examples of "internal transformations" versus "external righteousness."

3. Are we the "religious crowd" of our day? Are we drawing lines in the sand?

4. What do you enjoy more—the applause of people or the applause of heaven?

Prayer

"Search me, God, and know my heart; test me and know my anxious thoughts. See if there is any offensive way in me, and lead me in the way everlasting" (Ps. 139:23–24). I do not want to live my life playing the game of religion, saying the right things, going to the right places, convincing people of my righteousness. I confess to You I have nothing to offer except my failures and sin. Thank You for changing me forever by the sacrifice of Your Son's precious blood. I praise You for the constant work performed in the present by the Holy Spirit within me, conforming me to the image of Your dear Son. Forgive me for attempts to impress people. I long to hear from You, "Well done, good and faithful servant."

CHAPTER 10: RECKLESS GRACE

1. Read Matthew 8:1–3. The man with leprosy was desperate, suffering externally with sores and internally with shame. What did he ask Jesus? What was Jesus's response?

2. Do you have a faith like the leper—a faith knowing Jesus is always your only hope?

3. Do you spend time mainly with people just like you? Take a look around your circle of influence. Are there changes you need to make?

4. When Jesus established His church, He envisioned that His followers would live in such a way that hurting and broken people would come running to find a safe refuge. Is your church such a place?

Prayer

God, You made us all in Your image. "Red and yellow, black and white, they are precious in His sight." Make my eyes see others as only You would see them—not by their skin colors, job statuses, or achievements, but only as Your children. I am lost and aimless without You. Widen my heart and deepen my soul to have the faith of the leper. Lord, thank You for establishing the church to be a place of refuge. Use Your church to take care of the widows and the orphans, so that all who enter will automatically feel Your love through us.

CHAPTER 11: RADICAL HUMILITY

1. Do you suffer from a Messiah Complex? Can you think of stories played out in our society in which people seem to have a Messiah complex?

2. Do you struggle with pride? Nearly everyone does to some degree. What ways have you learned to deal with your pride? Do you have tools in place for when it surfaces in your life?

3. Satan is the father of lies. What lie is he telling you over and over again?

4. In God's kingdom, greatness is not about becoming more but about becoming less. Greatness is not measured by things acquired but by things given away. Greatness is not determined by status but by service. When you ponder those thoughts, what is God impressing upon you? What does He want you to give up? Who does He want you to serve?

Prayer

Jesus, You are the only Messiah I need in my life. You fulfill all my needs. Please lead me to people and places I could have never asked for or imagined. I need more of You and less of me. Take my pride and make it disappear. The only thing I want others to see in me is Your presence in the way I speak, serve, and study Your Word. I bow at Your feet, knowing You are the servant of all.

CHAPTER 12: MONKEY SEE, MONKEY DO

1. Is there someone you strive to imitate? Why did you choose that particular individual? What attributes does the person have that you want to emulate?

2. Read John 15:1–8. The word *remain* means to "continue to exist, especially after other similar or related people or things have ceased to exist." Jesus asks us to remain. Why do we have such a difficult time with this concept?

3. With God, all things are possible. Take a moment and reflect on the life of Paul. He persecuted Christians. What happened on the road to Damascus? What transformation happened that day? Have you had a similar experience? Or do you know someone who has?

4. Which do you spend more time and energy doing—learning to *know about Jesus* or learning to *know Jesus?*

Prayer

Lord, I desire to remain in You—to experience Your presence in my family life, my work life, my friend life, and every relationship I engage in. I look at the life of Paul, and it's so easy to point a finger and judge him for his choices. But the reality is, there is probably a little bit of Paul's heart in me. I am so grateful You chose to meet him on that Damascus road. Through Paul's writings, You have given Your children scriptures that give us hope and courage. Thank You for meeting me on my own Damascus road and for getting my attention in a way that led to life change. I will never be the same. Transform me day by day.

CHAPTER 13: WITH

1. What does your relationship with Jesus look like? Are you acquaintances, casual friends, close friends?

2. Do you view Jesus as an add-on feature? A drawer? An insurance policy? An audience? An instructor?

3. The word *intimacy* stirs up so many thoughts, feelings, and ideas. But Jesus wants an intimate relationship with you. What is standing in the way? Is it a person, place, or thing?

4. The God who created you in your mother's womb knows you best. Do you struggle to grasp that concept? If so, why isn't it enough for you to hear those words and accept them as a stamp on your heart?

Prayer

Recite Psalm 139 as a way to praise God for His understanding of who you are and as an invitation for Him to reveal His will to you.

CHAPTER 14: SOMETHING

1. What was the "something" about Jesus that got your attention?

2. Is there something about you that makes others want to be around you?

3. Do you know people like Paul, Chris and Randy, or Jenni, whose stories were presented in this chapter? There is something different about them that could have come only from their relationship with Jesus. Do you currently have people in your life whom you could imitate Jesus to?

4. We are called to "go and make disciples." Are you up for the challenge? What roadblocks do you need to remove in order to fulfill that command? What obstacles do you need to overcome so you can go and make disciples—fear, busyness, apathy?

Prayer

Jesus, there is something about You that I am drawn to. I am drawn to a heart that sees no limits. I am drawn to a Father who lovingly disciplines His children, for I do need correction. I am drawn to the Holy Spirit, who comforts me in all circumstances that cause me hurt and pain. I am drawn to the Savior, who asked the children to come to Him, for "the kingdom of heaven belongs to such as these." Draw me near. Make me holy. I desire to be an imitator of You. I want to love others all because You first loved me.

ACKNOWLEDGMENTS

Thank you. These words are truly insufficient, but none would be fully sufficient. So again, thank you. And these words are intended for many. To Keith, thank you for your honest and diligent editorial work. To Ingrid and the David C Cook team, thank you for joining me in this partnership. To Don, thank you for your professionalism and your encouragement along the way. To Alex, thank you for supporting me in this journey. Thank you to the many who have listened to these ideas and offered helpful insights. Thank you to those of you who have given me clear glimpses of who Jesus is and what He is like. Mostly, thank You, Jesus, for Your love and mercy.

ABOUT THE AUTHOR

Jamie Snyder is lead pastor of Lakeside Christian Church, where he preaches and teaches to thousands on a weekly basis. Though he has many titles—husband, father, preacher, writer, bookworm, table-tennis player extraordinaire—the most significant one, by far, is child of God. He resides with his wife and three children in Kentucky.

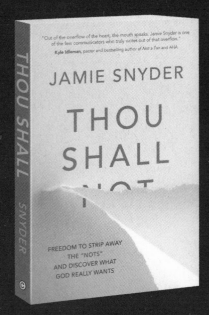